MW00947698

# THE
# FOUR R'S
## OF
# *Emmajoy*

# THE
# FOUR R'S
## OF
## *Emmajoy*

## MARY E. KROL

XULON ELITE

Xulon Press Elite
2301 Lucien Way #415
Maitland, FL 32751
407.339.4217
www.xulonpress.com

Unless otherwise indicated, Scripture quotations taken from the Holy Bible, New International Version (NIV). Copyright © 1973, 1978, 1984, 2011 by Biblica, Inc.™. Used by permission. All rights reserved.

Printed in the United States of America.

ISBN-13: 978-1-54567-489-5

IN THE EARLY YEARS OF THE NINETEEN-FIFTIES, Avon New York, was voted one of the most desirable cities to live in the United States. For me, nothing could have been further from the truth.

Children who are abused remain silent and suffer alone with thoughts and visions in their heads while their young hearts become hardened and confused because of someone else's sin.

This book is not written to expose how bad my childhood was, or how awful a mother or a parent can be, because Sigmund Freud could have a heyday with it. But it was written because of the freedom and redemption that has taken place over the past decades in my life.

These memoirs of my childhood tell of the harsh abusive sufferings my siblings and I suffered in the formative times of our lives. However the ending chapter, where I am an adult speaks of Redemption and how God is able to show love, forgiveness and mercy.

The characters names and the locations of events have been changed. Dates have also been changed to protect the innocent and the victims of my early life history. I have chosen my name to be Emmajoy.

# TABLE OF CONTENTS

# DEDICATION

I DEDICATE THIS BOOK TO MY BROTHER RONAN Daniel Regan. AKA, Arty. Despite his years of suffering, abuse and neglect, he has risen above his childhood maltreatment, and has become a wonderful brother, husband, father and grandfather. Against all odds, he has broken the chains of abuse and suffering. He defied the hatred and hurts of his past, and in its place he found and gave love. I love you Arty!

## Chapter One

# OVERCOMING

IT TOOK ME NEARLY FORTY YEARS TO COME TO A place where I was able to be free from emotional pain. I had decided a couple of decades before that, I would not let the wrecked childhood I had endured rule my thoughts, but in reality it did.

I can remember as far back to age three and having some emotional pain of my parents' divorce, but the pain grew deeper every year I got older. I hated the fact that my father had another family and what should have been mine, was given to his second family and I was only a part time receiver of seeing and being with my Dad.

Because of the divorce, adultery and anger of my parents, I suffered neglect and was robbed of the basic necessities of life. There was a disregard for my needs including; food shelter clothing love and affection. I often needed more medical care than I received, as I suffered from severe breathing problems including pneumonia. After time passed, my mother's depression and her husband's drinking robbed me of joy. At age seven I felt ugly, stupid and tired. I was physically and sexually abused. I usually had a serious look on my face as I was always worried about how would I was going to meet the demands of the day and care for myself and my siblings.

As a child, I never spoke to anyone of my abuse or needs. Silence remained on my lips as far as my home life was concerned. I never thought of myself as being anything other than the dirty little stupid girl from Autumn Avenue. Rats, roaches and roaming hands were always on my mind. But God had a different plan for me. As a child I had a strong faith and active prayer life. I would always pray for God to hear me and He did. So here I am now writing this book and overcoming emotional pain, finding forgiveness for my transgressors and living out my hope in Christ Jesus.

## Chapter Two

# HARRIET & NEIL

---

MY MOTHER, HARRIET MARGARET COOKE, WAS
a thin girl who had brown sparkling eyes, long straight brown hair
and a pretty smile. She was born in the mid 1930's, a time when
America was struggling to feed and employ its own people. She
smoked two packs of cigarettes a day. When I was ten, she told me
she had been a "serious smoker" since she was ten, but told me I
should never smoke because cigarettes were expensive.

Aunt Edna told me, my mother had been totally involved with
her family, but was jealous of many of her eleven siblings, and
often wallowed in gossip about them. When I became an adult,
Mom always told me whom she did and didn't like, down to every
last detail about why she didn't like them and Edna was right, Mom
was jealous.

My mother once told me as a child she dreamed of having
five sons and five dogs. Well she did have five sons, but she also
had two daughters. Two marriages and seven children consumed
her life.

My father Neil Liam Regan, was tall, lean and had green eyes and a great smile. He also smoked and he too was born in the '30's. He referred to his cigarettes as "coffin nails." He was very involved in his community life as he volunteered to coach the Catholic boys' basketball team and he was also a volunteer fireman.

Nanna Joy said they were a handsome couple, but I have never seen a picture of them together. They met in early winter in 1950 at the wedding of May & Paddy. You see May was Harriet's sister and Neil, was Paddy's brother. They danced to, "The Tennessee Waltz," by Patti Page. They had a unique situation, even after they divorced, my mother's ex-husband was also her brother in law.

Both of my parents were from large families. My mother had twelve siblings. There were nine sisters and three brothers. I knew them all. Harriet was the third youngest in the Cooke family.

In 2014, my great-niece put together a booklet with the Regan's family crest on the cover. It contained the history from the time of the Regan's arriving in the USA, to the present. It also had all the history of my father's parents, and his siblings and their families. She worked on the book for over one year accurately researching and documenting what she had found both in Ireland and the USA. My niece was able to trace our lineage back to the fifteenth century, and found our name came from a sect of Monks. She then had the beautifully documented book spiral bound and gave it to my father for his birthday. A few months later, she had a copy of the book made and gave it to me for my birthday. That book is one of the best gifts I have ever received!

My father was one of nineteen children, but the family shared two mothers. The first wife of my paternal grandfather became ill and died in her early thirties, so a cousin of the family was summoned by my grandfather from Ireland to come and help out the Regan family. Within two years of her arrival, she married my grandfather and completed the very large clan. Even though there were two mothers, there was no division in family bonding or in Irish looks. They were all of the same tribe. Neil was the third youngest in his family.

Unfortunately I never knew many of the Regan aunts, uncles or cousins.

So back to Harriet and Neil. It seems the couple continued to dance even after the wedding of their siblings and Harriet became pregnant in early 1951. They were both in high school so, of course, Harriet had to drop out of school, she was in the 10th grade, but Neil went on to graduate.

They were married by the Justice of the Peace in a civil ceremony, in City Hall, in August of 1951. Harriet wore a pretty silk pink dress, with a matching hat. Neil wore a clean pressed green suit. May and Paddy were their attendants. They were pronounced man and wife, Mr. and Mrs. Neil Regan! Harriet Regan was sixteen years old and Neil was seventeen. It was considered a mixed marriage because Harriet was Protestant and Neil was Catholic. Gasp! Well, so were May and Paddy.

They had a small reception at Harriet's parents' house and they all enjoyed homemade chocolate mayonnaise cake and coffee. Harriet's favorite sister, Edna made the cake. She always made the cakes. They again danced to Patsy Cline singing, "The Tennessee Waltz," on the old Victrola.

They moved into a tiny studio apartment on River Street in Avon. Avon was Harriet's hometown that overlooked the famous Long Creek River. The river was long and wide and powerful.

The river had much industry generated from its tidal waters from the mighty Atlantic Ocean. It was a beauty, full of barges and tourism and day liners. It was a profitable place to live and work. The city had about thirty-two thousand residents. It was a grand small city with great shops and many places of employment. It had ship yards where they produced WWII war ships. It was known for the perfection that came from its factories and brickyards. It was the home of a few National Landmarks. Avon had over one-hundred churches. Most of the residents walked to their places of employment and worship. It was a fine city.

Across the river was a smaller sleepy town where the Regan family had planted its roots and it was there Neil was able to find employment and studied to become an engineer for a drafting company. Each day he took the ferry to work and back for just a nickel.

In Nineteen fifty-one, Avon NY, was voted the most desirable USA city in which to live and raise a family. For me, nothing could have been further from the truth.

*Chapter Three*

# EMMA'S BIRTH

---

I WAS BORN IN LATE FALL AFTER A LONG AND DIF-ficult labor. My mother told me it was the most difficult birth of all of her seven children, as her labor was more than twenty-four hours long. I was also the smallest of all of her babies weighing in at five pounds, one ounce and sixteen inches long.

I was named after my two grandmothers, Emma & Joy. Emma, was Neil's mother's name and Joy, was Harriet's mother. So I became, Emma Joy. My family always called me, Emmajoy as if it was one name.

I was grand-child number forty-three of fifty-four on my maternal side of the family and the only one named after my grand-mothers. In mid-December of 1951, I was baptized as a Roman Catholic in St. Luke's Church, in Avon NY.

My mother confessed to me that in my first months of life, she didn't know how to care for me and didn't know how to stop me from crying. She told me she didn't want to be a bad mother, but really did not know how to care for a baby. She said I was always crying. So she would give me bottle after bottle of evaporated milk with sugar water to keep me from crying, and I always drank them. At age one I weighed thirty pounds! I walked at nine months and was talking in sentences at twelve months.

Mom told me I was born an "old soul," who liked to hang around older people rather than play with my cousins. I never really enjoyed playing with dolls or dirt. I much preferred cleaning house or washing clothes. Things such as dirt, dust and disorder disturbed me and I would have to fix what was out of place. At the age of five, I would babysit two and three year olds and take proper care of them My aunts and uncles always told me I was the smartest of all the cousins because I remembered details and events even from age two. They would often quiz me by asking, what did Nanna Joy wear on Christmas day when I was I two, and I could recall vividly details, not just of Nanna, but others too. Having such a memory can be a blessing or a curse. Either way, I can recall many, many memories of my life.

I had one aunt who reminded me that I was able to cross the street and go to the store to buy my mother's cigarettes at age three…Oh my… can you imagine? I do remember doing that, but my mother watched me cross the street in front of the house. When I returned, I would yell for, "Mommy" until she came out front to watch me cross back over the road. I was always afraid to cross the street if I wasn't at a crosswalk. Needless to say, there was not a crosswalk in font of our house. I also remember picking our neighbors flowers on the way to the store. They were tulips. I picked all twenty five of them, but just the petals and left the stems. I threw the petals on the street in front of me as I pretended I was getting married. Later on in life I became a member of the same church as the woman whose flowers I had picked. She had remembered and recognized me…ugh! She came up to me and said, "Are you the Emmajoy who left my stems." "Yes I am." I said. She often reminded me of my "pickings".

*Chapter Four*

# THE HOUSE

SHORTLY AFTER MY FIRST BIRTHDAY WE LEFT River Street and moved into my maternal grandparent's house on Autumn Avenue. It was just a few short blocks from where we had lived near the river.

The house was an eighty year old large four story brick house like many of the brownstones in New York City, but it lacked the ornate touches of the gilded craftsman. It sat on top of a very large hill. The house had a massive concrete front porch with many steps which led to the large solid- wood front door. A door that was rarely used by family or friends. As a child I was convinced it was really a door just for company and for Aunt Sue. Aunt Sue was a proper lady and always used the front door. Sue was Joy's sister. She came often to see our Grandpa, as he was her father. The rest of the family used the back door or the downstairs front door.

The house had endless stairs and great "to slide down banisters." The woodwork was massive and dark. The floors were all dark wood too, except for my grandmother's apartment which was carpeted and had white painted woodwork. Even though there were three apartments in the house, it was treated as one big dwelling, no locked doors or separation. The house had nine bedrooms but only two bathrooms, and both had claw footed tubs. No showers, just baths.

The hallways were poorly lit, but there always seemed to be enough lighting in the living areas. It was an eerie house, void of color. The hallways were long and each hallway housed a dresser. The windows on the main floor were ten feet tall. Closets were sparse both in clothing and in number, except on the fourth floor. That closet had an entrance and an exit and was two rooms long. We all stored our winter things there and it reeked of mothballs. The fourth floor had five bedrooms and a breezeway. It also had a beautiful breezeway staircase that led to a large skylight, where the older children climbed up into and played on the roof.

The house was always too hot or too cold. Gas space heaters were used to heat the massive house. The house also had large wrought iron ornate grates on the floors that had "open and close" vents to allow the heat in. We used them to allow conversation in, or to watch what was going on in the floor below us. As a child it was always intriguing to listen to the adults talk, but just when you thought you were safe to spy, an aunt or uncle would step under the vent, announce your name and demand you close the vent and "get to work." Well we didn't have jobs, but we knew what "get to work" meant, so we would step away and make noises as if we were doing something useful, like moving a chair as we were pretending to sweep the floor.

The furniture was sparse, but we had what we needed. There were no pictures, knickknacks or signs of artwork anywhere in the house, but there were doilies on my grandmother's furniture.

Every couch pulled out to a bed and there were always plenty of bed linens for those curling up on the floor. Without a doubt, there was always a visiting relative spending the night and one or more of us kids gave up our bed and slept on the floor so the guest could have the bed.

We had one telephone in the house and that was on the bottom floor. When I was three years old I called my Uncle Rob at two AM. "Uncle Rob, the house is on fire and everybody is sleeping." It was not on fire. Uncle Rob, who lived six houses from us, came racing over in his car. It was the first and only time I saw Uncle Rob in his pajamas. Needless to say everyone was now awake, so we all had hot tea and toast. Nanny Joy thanked God the house was on fire. I was told to never use the phone again, but of course I did. I remember one time I actually called the operator and asked her about her family. She was kind and answered a few of my questions, but then politely told me she had to hang up as she, "had work to do." I loved talking on the telephone, but no one ever called me. I still remember our four digit phone number. The phone didn't have a rotary dial, you just picked up the phone and like magic, the operator was there. She would say, "Number please." Then you would tell her the number you wanted, and if you were unsure of the number, she would always look it up for you. All of the operators were female.

We had three large dining room tables and twenty six chairs and the kids only sat at the table for meals. Kids sat on the floor if we were in the house. We ate in shifts, first the kids and then the adults. When the kids were finished eating we then went into the kitchen, to clean the dishes and pots and pans from our meal.

We had a lot of deliveries on Autumn Avenue. We had the bread man, the milk man, the egg man and on and on. On any given day we consumed four gallons of milk, five loaves of bread, three dozen eggs, two boxes of cereal, twenty pounds of potatoes and several pounds of vegetables and meat. If it was macaroni day, Aunt Edna cooked six pounds. Each day's left overs were the next day's lunch. We also had mail delivered twice a day.

There always seemed to be a lot of food in the house, yet, as a child, I was always hungry. Food and servings were rationed except for one cousin who would eat anything not locked up. He would even take food off of your plate while you were eating.

All of the unmarried siblings of my mother and two of her married siblings, along with their families lived in that house. The owners, my Nanna Joy, and Grandpa (with the cane) and my maternal great-grandfather all lived in that house too. My grandmother's father was referred to as "Grandpa with the chair," because he was wheel chair bound. As kids we would secretly try to ride in his Franklin Delano Roosevelt style wheel chair up and down the long hallways of the house, but, the big "wheel noise" on the wooden floor always gave us away. The wheelchair had an oversized wicker cane high back seat without arm rests and wooden wheels. Our other grandfather, (Joy's husband) was referred to as "Grandpa with the cane," because that's what he used. In all I think we were twenty-one people living there and "All" the family visited every Sunday for dinner. We would often have 50 or more people in our house for our Sunday, after church meal.

At Christmastime, we only had one tree in the house and the nine foot tree was always placed in my Grandmother's apartment in front of the tall left hand window. It was decorated with beautiful glass ornaments and large colored bulbs that were hot to the touch. It was adorned with hundreds of strands of tinsel. Under the Christmas tree skirt, the tree was housed in a giant tub of water, that was checked twice a day and kept half full at all times.

All of the gifts for the adults would be placed under the tree, but all of the kid's gifts were placed on the couch or in the living room chairs. Our Christmas stockings would be stuffed with oranges, tangerines, candy canes and nuts. All of the children had a stocking with their name on the white top part of the boot shaped felt stocking. We never saw the tree decorated before Christmas, because Santa decorated it when he delivered the gifts. We were allowed to hang one ornament on the tree to remind Santa and his reindeer to stop for us. Every Christmas Eve, Santa stopped at our house and we believed with his secret hand wave, he decorated our tree, left us gifts and in the morning, we were he recipients of his beautiful magic!

That house, in my early years, had many great memories. We had weddings, birthdays, showers, good company, good meals, great fellowship and even our relatives lying in repose, on Autumn Ave.

We would see great parades on Main St. on Memorial Day, and we would wave American flags and salute those in the line of march. We would then meet with my mother's family and their friends' for a picnic in the local county park, where there would sometimes be two hundred people in our clan. On that big day our older cousins would walk three miles to the outskirts of the city at six AM to reserve our fieldstone covered picnic area. Each picnic house had a huge fieldstone fireplace and large table. Arty and I were convinced the Indians built the houses. After all the park was Mohawk Grounds.

It was such a fun park, there was a large fieldstone floor wading pool, which was spring fed. There we would catch pollywogs and tiny craw fish. My uncles would place our one dozen large watermelons under a nearby running stream so they would be nice and cold when we were ready to sprinkle them with salt and eat them. The park had a large baseball field, so of course there was always a game to be played. Teams were picked, but there was really no division, we just cheered for everyone. Many of the clan would play cards or throw horseshoes. I can still remember the sound of the metal horseshoe being pitched and hitting the post while the thrower yelled, "Ringer."

Food was always aplenty that day and my mother always made the baked beans. She always made sure we were clean and had something nice to wear. I loved holidays!

Memorial Day was always a delicious day. Every family bought at least two covered dishes. Potato and macaroni salads along with coleslaw were in endless supply. There were always special treats at the picnic like soda, potato chips and cupcakes. Hot dogs, hamburgers and barbecue chicken were also served and there was always enough for seconds. Salads sat out for hours and nobody ever got sick.

I loved Memorial Day, as it was a great family day. My family always showed respect by visiting gravesites and placing wreaths of the members of our family who were deceased, who had served in the military. At the picnic site, we always had a word of prayer given by the oldest son of Nanna Joy.

I went to my family picnics for the first twelve years of my life, then many of the family members moved away and the picnics gently faded away.

*Chapter Five*

# TROUBLE WITH THE "WALTZ"

---

IN 1952 IN THE MIDDLE OF NOVEMBER, NEIL
took a job as a part-time bar tender to help make ends meet. The
bar was just a stone's throw from the house on Autumn Ave. He
was working full time at the drafting company and also studying to
become an engineer. Harriet found out she was pregnant with their
second child and this baby was due in early summer.

It was common rumor that Neil had been seen with other women
in the bar and was having an affair with a women from Ohio, whose
name was, Ida. I remember she had a loud high pitched voice that
made your ears sting when she spoke. She was lean and wore bright
red lipstick. She was the first vegetarian I knew. She never wore
stockings, which was quite unusual for a woman at that time.

And so the rocky road my parents limped on became broken
beyond repair. The marriage was crumbling faster than week old
uncovered baked goods. But in the meantime, Harriet was preparing
to give birth, and in the early days of June 1953 she gave birth to
my brother, Ronan Daniel Regan. We just called him, "Arty."

Later in life, my mother told me my father didn't even want to give her a ride home from the hospital after she and Ronan were discharged. He didn't want to have anything to with us. But he did pick her up from the hospital, drove her to the front door of the big house on Autumn Ave., and told her to, "Get out." He never even opened the door for her while she was struggling to get out of the car with their newborn son and diaper bag. I was angry she told me this as I really wanted to see him through rose colored glasses, never having a fault.

On the other hand, the whole family was there to support my mother and her new baby. My Mom said I was so anxious to see this new baby I was getting, I could hardly contain myself. While waiting for her to unwrap him in his yellow blanket. I kept hollering "Hurry up, hurry up." When she finally had him unwrapped I looked at him and said, "Oh, that's all?" She said "Yes." She then offered to sit with me and let me hold him, so we did and then she said, I bit him. I was twenty months old. I had teeth, lots of teeth.

Within the next few months, my father was seen with his girl-friend, Ida everywhere in town. When one of uncles who lived with us on Autumn Avenue found out about my father's affair, he took it upon himself to gather my father's belongings and throw them onto the street. When Dad came home from work that afternoon he picked them up, put them in his car and never returned to Autumn Ave. He never returned even to pick up my brother and me for visitation. When Arty was baptized at St. Luke's Church, my father had made all of the arrangements through his priest friend, and my mother on the telephone. He then met us at the church.

Mom said he rented a room here and there, for a bit, but eventually moved back to Bridgetown, his family's town across the river.

He then filed for divorce on the grounds of adultery admitting he was the guilty one.

For visitations, a family member, usually an uncle or older cousin would walk with me to the ferry, where I would ride across the river by myself to see my father for the weekends. He would always meet me at the ferry dock with his car. "How you doing?" he would ask. I was always, "Just fine." I was three years old! Other passengers on the ferry watched out for me, sometimes even holding my hand while we took the ten minute journey to the East side of the creek. I always made the return trip by myself. Often when I returned from Bridgetown, no one was there to meet me at the ferry, so I would walk up the very large hill to the house on Autumn Ave., by myself.

I can still hear the ferry boat whistle, along with the massive chains being pulled by men to help launch the boat and I can smell the fuel used to move the large vessel from shore to shore. I can feel the wind on my face from the outside deck in the warmer weather and I can remember the heat from the small potbelly coal stove inside the cabin during the colder months. I can also feel the "thump" as the boat docked as it came to a standstill, so I could depart from each of my many transports across the mighty river. The ferry was a happy place for me, as I knew every trip was bringing me to see my mother or my father.

But times were changing, Mom wouldn't get out of bed. I was usually hungry, and Arty was dirty, hungry and crying and everybody always seemed to be yelling. I tried to take care of him, but I was too little. Even this "old soul" was too young to care for her mother and her brother. When I tried to do motherly tasks for Arty and me an aunt would yell and state, "That's your Mother's job." And then, she would yell at my mother, but she didn't get out of bed.

The Tennessee Waltz was over, the Victrola was making a scratchy noise and I missed my father.

Later in my life, I realized this was the most devastating situation my mother had faced in her short life. She was truly in love with my father, and she was now faced with the demise of their marriage. She had lost her love. She now lived with feelings of rage that came with the betrayal of her marriage. She had the weight of being a single teenage parent with two children in 1953, and that, gave birth to her anger and depression.

Deep down my Mom was a kind soul who would do anything she could to help you, including fixing your toaster. She was very mechanical and intelligent. She eventually found her expression of love and it came through the love of animals, mostly dogs.

*Chapter Six*

# THE BEGINNING OF
# THE SECOND FAMILY

---

IN MAY OF 1955 MY FATHER MARRIED THE GAL
Ida, from Ohio, he had been dating. She was pregnant with his
child. They were married in a Catholic Church by a priest in,
Massachusetts. The priest was a personal friend of my father.
He was the same priest who had baptized Arty and me. The pictures I saw of the wedding were lovely. Ida wore a beautiful
white Cinderella ballroom style gown and the groom and all his
groomsmen had white tuxedos. The wedding party was very large.
Sixteen attendants counting the flower girl and ring bearer. I did
not go the wedding. Arty and I were not invited. But then Arty was
almost two and I was three and a half. I was mad. I didn't quite
understand was a wedding was, I only knew my father was going
to a party and I was not.

The new Mr. and Mrs. Neil Regan, moved into a relative's
house in Bridgetown and lived on the top floor apartment. Within
two years they had two babies, both girls. Their first daughter was
named Nancy Lynn and the second child was Anna Lynn. They

eventually had a third daughter and named her Tammy Lynn. A few years after her birth they had a son and he was named after our father, Neil Liam Jr. Three years later Ida, gave birth to Kevin.

My mother told me they were never legally married because he married Ida in May of '55 and their divorce didn't become final until August of '55. So that could be why they married in Massachusetts. The Catholic Church never recognized the marriage of my parents, (because they were married in a civil ceremony), but New York State did.

When I was six and my brother Arty and I were fully doing the every other weekend divorce visit on Sunday 'til six PM thing. So we hopped the ferry on Friday afternoons and we arrived at my father's house in time for dinner. Food glorious food! My father would often be too busy to pick us up at the ferry, so we would walk nearly two miles to his house.

Ida never sat down at the table to eat with us, she stayed in the kitchen eating her kidney and string beans out of the cans, and we didn't care. There were three meals a day and a snack before bedtime! On Autumn Avenue, people and times were changing, we rarely had more than two meals a day, and the servings were limited. When the father of the family is absent, everything changes. In Bridgetown we were full. We even got to walk to our uncle's grocery store and pick out a pint of our favorite ice cream. Arty and I both loved butter pecan.

My father would come home for dinner, but that was about it. He worked three jobs trying to support his growing family. He worked as an engineer, he worked in his brother's grocery store in the evening and on weekends he drove a taxi on the graveyard shift. He was a good provider, but as a father he was absent.

In the early 1960's my father bought a big house in his hometown for his family. All of his second family children went to private schools and he never missed his child support payment to my mother. His children all owned three pair of shoes and had boots! They all had clean nice clothing hanging in their closets and when they dressed, they had several dresses to choose from. They had dressers that had socks, underwear and nice sweaters folded neatly in their drawers. They all had their own bed. On Autumn Ave., we slept two or three in a bed, even the adult sisters. I thought my father was rich.

Early on, it was very evident Ida, didn't like my brother Arty. She hated our neglect, and screamed at us about it many times. "Why are you so dirty? Why don't you get your hair cut? Why don't you get yourself a decent pair of shoes," and it continued on and on. She was always screaming at us. She would yell at us about our mother, saying, "What does that slob do with the money I send you?" Her yelling took us straight to the depths of hell, as did the neglect we suffered on a daily basis from our mother. It ruined our self-esteem. It deposited in us anger, hate and rage. Was it worth a weekend of having food to have to listen to this raging maniac? Did she not realize how out of control she was? She herself was full of the evils she planted and reaffirmed in us every other weekend. She told us, she was, "Too embarrassed to have us meet the rest of the Regan family because we wore filthy rags." I cried in secret for hours as her statement affirmed in me I was the ugly dirty stupid kid from Autumn Avenue. When my father heard of this he took us to a department store and bought us new clothing. Arty and I also got new shoes and coats. We were so happy! Well, we were happy on Saturday, but on Sunday when it was time for us to catch the ferry we learned we had to leave our new clothing and shoes in Bridgetown.

Arty was one of those children, (especially boys) who were born with an immature ureter, and he wet the bed. Unfortunately not one of the two mothers he had, understood or had compassion for him regarding this matter. Ida would wake him at eleven PM and change his bed, wash his sheets and give him an ice cold bath. She would repeat the process at three AM, but at three AM, she would also beat him. After his ice cold bath, she would beat him with anything she could reach. Be it a hairbrush a belt or her hand. No matter; she beat him. She woke all of us to watch the vivid display of demonic behavior. There we were, Emmajoy, age nine, Nancy Lynn, age five and Anna Lynn age three, all watching this screaming maniac beat and abuse my seven year old brother. My heart was aching and crying on the inside, but on the outside, I had to be stoic and pretend I agreed with her for fear of getting beat myself. She would scream in her high pitched, ear piercing voice, "This is what will happen to you if you wet the bed…do you hear me?" Each one of us would have to acknowledge her by saying out loud "Yes," as she would not accept a head nod. Even Anna Lynn the three year old had to say yes, and she was still wearing diapers to bed at night. Ida tried to put a diaper on Arty, but it was too small. He got hit for that too. There was no way the neighbors didn't hear her. There was no one to help. Arty was in the same prison of abuse on both sides of the river. My father was not home, he was busy driving the taxi, trying to help ends meet, to buy things like hair brushes, belts and diapers.

Several years passed and slowly the every other weekend visits become less and less frequent, and we finally didn't go at all. It didn't matter. Our father was never there anyway.

Ida and my father divorced after seventeen years of marriage. He soon found Betsy. He cashed in our life insurance policies to buy her a house. Well their relationship lasted only a few years. The same month he moved out of Betsy's house, he moved in with a women from a distant town and married her a few months later. They remained married until his death.

Ida never allowed her children to visit us in Avon. She made it very clear the Regan kids were never to go to Avon to see Arty or me. I don't think her kids ever rode the ferry. As kids we just accepted it.

Ida died in her early fifties from an incurable dreadful disease. When I told Arty she had died, he said, "It couldn't happen to a better person." Arty never spoke ill of anyone.

## Chapter Seven

# I'M SORRY ARTY

---

AS YOU KNOW MY FIRST INTRODUCTION TO Arty was when I was a twenty month old toddler. When I was in the oral stage, and I bit Arty. And unfortunately that stayed with me for the first fifteen years of my life. I was always doing something to hurt Arty.

Arty was a small, boy, with blond hair, brown eyed and a mischievous but sweet nature. He always had a bandage on his body either afflicted by me, or by scaling a large fence or walls and not quite making it to the top. He had the "Tom Sawyer" look, but without the hat. He was not an "old soul" as I was, as he enjoyed playing outside with our cousins, eating dirt and swinging on ropes. He played kick the can, softball and hide and go seek. He was very active and athletic.

When Arty first attended school, I, being the big sister, walked with him and showed him where to go. Our mother did not take him. "Go with Emmajoy," she told him. I was two grades ahead of him. He was in kindergarten, I was in second grade. He caught on very quickly and soon didn't need an escort. He found his own small group of boys to hang with and didn't need his "old soul sister/mother" looking after him. He always walked or ran faster than me anyway, so I was glad that, "I was rid of him." Even though he was faster than me, he slowed me down because I felt I had to watch his every move to keep him safe while we were on the street.

Arty was not well cared for by my mother at all. In fact it pains me to say she abused him. Physically and emotionally, this child was neglected. We all knew he wet the bed, and my mother did not see to his needs concerning his clothing or his bedding. No plastic mattress and no set of sheets, or pillow. He had a set of sheets, but she took them away, because she said she had better things to do than wash wet sheets every day. She didn't see to it that he was properly bathed. He didn't own a toothbrush. He never visited the dentist as a child, yet he had the best smile ever!

He was often sent to bed without his supper for something he didn't do, or sent to bed because our mother didn't want to, "look at him." I knew he was hungry and thirsty but yet again, I had to side with the adult, the one in authority, the one in charge. She was the one you had to listen to and obey even when you knew she was wrong. I took her side because I didn't want to be thirsty or hungry as we were experiencing more and more hunger every week, and If Arty goes to bed, I won't have to look at him either.

When Arty was in kindergarten, the school nurse called me into her office to ask me a few questions about him. She asked me if Arty had any problems at home and did he have enough to eat, did he sleep on the floor, in a bed or with someone else, and many other questions. I was nervous, but I finally answered all the questions she asked and I thought, great someone is going to help us! Maybe they will help Mom get out of bed. We will get food and toilet paper. Yahoo… I won't have to wash my own clothing. Then she said to me, "I have never smelled you, but your brother smells like "urine" and his clothing is too big. Tell your mother to take care of him, and don't come back to school until he is taken care of." We both were also loaded with bedbug bites, but she didn't say anything about that as I stood there scratching my arms until they bled. I am now sick to my stomach thinking my brother is sick and dying because he smelled like, "urine." I didn't know what urine was, ( I remember what she said by these words as "your in trouble") I didn't know what it caused, but I remembered the nurse said, "urine" and now I have to go home and tell my mother my brother is sick with "urine" and he can't go back to school until he's better. Maybe that's why he's so skinny. He has "urine." I didn't dare tell anyone in my class, but my day was ruined, and I could tell all of the teachers were taking about my brother and me, by the way they were looking at me. My heart was heavy. Maybe I should pretend I'm sick and go home early to tell my mother. I wanted Arty to get help. I didn't like him, but I loved him. Maybe I too should be checked for "urine."

I didn't go home early that day, but on the way home I rehearsed what I needed to tell my mother... The school nurse said Arty is sick and needs to see a doctor. No that wasn't right, she never took us to the doctors. Maybe if I told her Arty had a funny smell she would get him checked. Well, maybe not; she smelled funny too. I know, I'll tell her Arty and I have "urine" and the nurse wants us get fixed before we come back to school. After all, that is what the nurse said. I thought if I included myself in the sickness, Arty would have a better chance of being seen, as she usually took better care of me than him. Maybe Nanna Joy would take us to the doctor. I'll say a prayer to God and ask Him to help us.

I finally reached home and there my mother was asleep in her fourth floor bedroom in the dark. "Mom are you sleeping?" I said. "Well why else would I be in bed." She yelled out. "Well I have something to tell you." My "old soul mother role" went right into action. "You need to get out of bed and take Arty to the doctors because the school nurse said he has "urine" and he can't come back to school until he's taken care of." I didn't mention the school nurse had interrogated me or that she thought Arty's clothing was too big. "And I want to be checked for "urine" too," I told her.

She got out of bed and she was madder than a wet hen, yelling and screaming, but that seemed to be her expected behavior. Vulgar words; words that I never heard before were spewing from her mouth. She was angry, or worse yet, "Mad." "What are you trying to say?" Do you mean urine as in peeing your pants and bed?" "Well you should smell like urine if you wet the bed." I now understood what "Your In" meant. I didn't need to be checked. My mother sent him to school the next day, in the same clothing he slept in and this would go on for days until she got out of bed to wash our clothing. I felt sorry for Arty and I promised myself I would try to do more laundry for him, but I didn't.

Funny how there were always mounds of laundry, but we never had anything nice to wear. Most of our clothing was hand me downs from our endless number of cousins. Her sisters stepped in a bit to help us, but most of them worked, and Edna was the one that stayed home and took care of her own four children and cooked for all the rest of the families that lived on Autumn Avenue.

Arty got a beating that night, he didn't have any dinner, and she didn't bath him or give him a change of clothing. It wasn't his first beating, nor would it be the last. I could hear her yelling as she beat him, "Don't you ever let that school nurse near you again…do you hear me…do you hear me?" I didn't hear Arty answer, but after several minutes the beating stopped and she came into the kitchen and announced, "No food for him and don't give the little brat any-thing to drink because he will only wet the bed again." Mom sat at the kitchen table and lit and smoked a cigarette in anger. "Emmajoy, make me a cup of coffee." I immediately started to perk a fresh pot of coffee for her.

Again that night, Arty wet the bed and in the morning, he went to school with his large smelly clothing. The nurse sent a note home with me with the same concerns, but my mother never addressed the issue. She just beat Arty again. The school nurse asked me if I gave the note to my mother, I replied "Yes," but I also asked her to please leave Arty alone. She never talked to me about him again.

About a week later Mom told Arty to take a bath. He got yelled at because he didn't know how to adjust the faucets to control the water temperature. So our mother did go into the bathroom to show him how to use the faucets, but it cost him a whack to his head. When he got into the bath tub, I heard him crying, because he didn't know how to wash himself. "Emmajoy, learn me to wash so mommy doesn't get mad again." I showed him how to wash and told him to wash his face first, to which he replied, "If I wash my face first, I won't be able to see what I'm doing." He was so vulnerable sitting in that tub shivering because the water was to cold, I cried. I made the water warmer and then I showed him how to wash and rinse. We didn't have any clean towels, because, of course, Mom didn't do the laundry, so Arty dried off with his dirty shirt. I don't remember what he put on after his bath, but he sure did smell nice and clean.

A few months passed and we were getting ready to celebrate Thanksgiving. We were looking forward to the extra food we would have, and especially to having fresh fruit in the house. That was a real treat! We usually had a few apples, as they were the least expensive, but I don't remember anytime except Christmas and Thanksgiving when we had other fresh fruits. This time I had an orange, Nanna Joy had saved it for me! If I didn't keep it hidden, someone would surely take it, so I put it in my grandmother's underwear drawer. Surely it will be safe there. I told Arty," Nanna Joy gave me an orange and we are going to eat it later before we go to bed. It will make up for the cold bath and whack you got to your head when you were learning to wash." He smiled and gave me a love hit. I told him where the orange was, but not to touch it. I would get it when we were ready to eat it. He agreed.

Later in the day Arty was outside playing and fell and scraped his knees, but worst of all he ripped his pants. He didn't have play clothes and school clothes to change into, he wore the same outfit for the better part of a week. But, there he was, missing the fabric of both knees of his trousers. He knew he was in trouble, and so did I. Mom was going to beat the stuffing out of him and we both knew it. We went into the house and had supper and she didn't seem to notice. Good.

As we were getting ready to climb to the fourth floor of the house to go to bed, I stopped in Nanna Joy's apartment to retrieve the most awaited orange. My mother was there, talking with her mother. I went to the dresser, took out the orange and my mother asked, "Where are you going with that?" "Nanna Joy gave me the orange and Arty and I are going to eat it before we go to sleep." She took the orange from me, took us up to the fourth floor, beat Arty for ripping his pants and told him he couldn't have any of the orange. She beat him with her shoe. He was crying pretty hard, and after she put her shoe back on, she smacked him in his face and told him to, "Be quiet." His cries echoed through the big house.

Arty stayed in bed, but she took me back down stairs to my grandmother's apartment where we ate the orange. I had a hard time swallowing it as that orange was supposed to be for Arty and me. Nanna Joy said to my mother, "Why do you always hit the boy like that?" Mom lit and smoked a cigarette in anger. I went to bed.

In the back of the house on Autumn Ave., there was a large court yard. It was made up of the back yards of four city blocks. Rarely did any cars go in the courtyard as our house was the only place that had a driveway access to the area, hence it was our play area. If we were out playing, chances are we were in the courtyard. On any given day, counting my cousins and all the neighborhood kids we had two teams of anything we wanted to play. Softball, football, dodgeball, you name the game, we had the kids.

One day we were playing softball and my cousin Kenny hit a grand slam for our team! I never played, but I was always an "extra." He hit the ball right over one of the neighbor's fence. Arty ran to retrieve it. He scaled the fence wall without any problem on the way over, but on the way back he caught his leg on the fence post and he ripped the skin of his shin clear down to the bone. He was bleeding and hurting. He couldn't walk. "Don't tell my mother," were the first words out of his mouth. We all agreed; we would not tell. A few of my cousins carried him to the house and put him in Kenny's room on the third floor, after all it was Kenny's fault he got hurt in the first place, because he's the one who hit the ball over the fence. Mom usually didn't go to the apartment on the third floor, so we should be safe. We got Arty to the third floor bedroom and washed his wounds and put toilet paper on his leg. It didn't work. His wound was still bleeding. We searched everywhere, but we couldn't find any bandages anywhere in the house and all the band aids we had were too small. Arty was hurting, but all he kept saying was, "Please don't tell my mother." Finally we taped a women's personal hygiene item to his leg with electric tape. That worked. I prayed for Arty that he wouldn't lose his leg or die.

By now it is suppertime and Aunt Edna was calling for us to come and eat. You know it's going to be a good supper if Aunt Edna cooked and we might even have some gelatin with evaporated milk, or cake for desert. We all sat down to eat and Aunt Edna said, "Where's Arty?" Arty was Aunt Edna's favorite. We all just looked at each other. No one wanted to speak up. She asked the same question again, "Where's Arty?" Kenny piped up and quickly cried out, "He's in my bed and he broke his leg." My mother and her sisters run up three flights of stairs, (we all followed) and found Arty in Kenny's bed in pain and still bleeding from his leg. Aunt Edna, removed the dressing and gasped, "Dear God we can see his bones, call for an ambulance." but my mother said, "No, he will be fine." Aunt Edna then screamed, "Get me some healing ointment and go to the drug store and get me large bandages," Edna's husband followed all of her command and was back within 20 minutes and tended to Arty's wound. I heard Edna whisper to my mother, "Harriet, you are unfit." Mom just watched Aunt Edna take care of Arty from the doorway of the bedroom while she smoked her cigarette. Arty had supper in Kenny's bed that night. Aunt Edna changed the bandages and nursed the wound for Arty every day, she even made him, his own chocolate mayonnaise cake. Our mother made him walk on it and go to school. He limped and refrained from sports for six months, but he did not get a beating for it. Perhaps she saw that he had suffered enough.

The day after Arty's injury, a few of us, went back to the place where he hurt his leg. We saw there was still blood and skin on the fencepost. After that, we treated that particular part of the fence as it was a shrine, like a tribute to Arty. We all looked at the remnants from Arty's wound and had a moment of silence.

Arty and I always had to do the dishes after supper. I washed, he dried. We would also use the time to practice our singing. We both sang well and we harmonized with one another. It was a sort of bonding time for us, for about ten minutes.

One particular evening, we are doing our chores. I'm washing and Arty is drying the dishes, but he was a little slower than me and the dish strainer was filling up quickly. Well sure enough a glass fell off the strainer and crashed to the floor and of course broke into a few dozen pieces. I hate cleaning up broken glass, as it seems you never get it all on the first sweep. " I command you to sweep the floor and pick up all the broken glass Arty," to which he replied, "Nope you made it fall, you sweep it up." Well he was right. If I had just waited a few minutes to finish washing, the accident would not have happened. But on the other hand I wasn't going to let Arty tell me what to do. I insisted he clean it up, but, he insisted he wasn't going to. Well I couldn't leave a broken glass on the floor, so I sweep it up and then sweep again to make sure there are no slivers left on the floor. I slowly put the broom away and then grabbed Arty by the neck, pushed him into the bathroom and flushed his head in the toilet. Mom heard the commotion and hollered down stairs, "What are you two doing down there?" To which I answer, "Nothing! I'm flushing Arty's head in the toilet," to which she replied, "Oh."

Another time we were downstairs doing the dishes and Arty and I had an argument over whether or not it was going to rain the next day. Because we couldn't agree on the forecast, I made him brush his teeth in the dirty dish water, with the sponge I used to clean the dishes. "There now your face is wet so you don't have to worry about tomorrow's rain." I was turning into my mother and I hated it, but I couldn't stop. Lord, help me!

We were now living in a much smaller house because someone made a serious financial mistake and my Grandmother's house was foreclosed on. Autumn Ave., was gone. So after the tooth washing, I tried to avoid Arty, but we lived with one another in the small house, so it was difficult to do.

While preparing to write this book I asked Arty if he wanted me to put in any particular story in it to which he replied, "I don't have any memory of my childhood until I was nine." He then told me this story. "I was sent to the store to get Mommy her cigarettes and newspaper. She gave me 40 cents. My shoes were too big not to mention the left one had a rip on the side and the right one had a big hole on the bottom and I was sick and tired of it. I decided I was going to go to the shoemaker and get my shoes fixed, even if it cost me a beating. And so I did. They fixed them while I waited. First they fixed the rip with shiny new heavy black rope type thread, and then they cut out a piece of leather and glued it to the right bottom. I gave the shop owner twenty cents. I then went to the store and bought the cigarettes for Mom. I thought for sure I would get a beating with my repaired shoes when I got home, but I didn't. Was Mom having a change of heart?"

Within three short years of getting his shoes repaired under his own initiative, Arty moved into Aunt Edna's house when he was only twelve years old. He put his very few belongings into a pillow case and walked to his new residence. No one seemed to care. I guess he was tired of the beatings. He never returned home. After he graduated from high school, he left the state. I love you Arty.

## Chapter Eight

# NORMAN

IN LATE 1955 MY MOTHER MET OUR NEIGHBOR'S friend who worked with him in the local construction company. His name was, Norman MacCarthy O'Sullivan Fitzgerald. Second generation in the USA, of Irish decent. He referred to himself as an Irish Mick and wanted to be called, Norm. Well we could call him Norm, but he was not normal.

They soon started to date and were married in May of 1956. Arty and I were not invited to that wedding either, nor did we see any pictures. They were married at a friend's house by a Justice of the Peace. Norm suggested we could call him "Daddy Norm," but somehow, it could never roll off my tongue, so he was just Norman. He was eleven years older than our mother.

Compared to my father he was a homely man. He had a sort of leprechaun look…big nose and pointy ears. He liked to watch Saturday morning cartoons and laugh at silent films. He was a nail bitter. He bit his nails to the nubs. His father was 6'4" and his mother was 4'9." He was 5'7"with a small frame. He was a man who liked to play baseball, gamble, drink whiskey and watch sports on television. He managed money poorly. He had gone to a monastery straight out of high school to become a Jesuit Priest, but that didn't work out. He had been married before, but divorced several years before he met our mother. He didn't have any children.

When he married my mother, he referred to her as his "bride" and called her that until the day he died. She hated it. Harriett Margaret Cooke Regan, was now Mrs. Norman MacCarthy O'Sullivan Fitzgerald. Whew...try writing that three time fast! They were married for thirty nine years.

They took a five day honeymoon in upstate New York and Arty and I stayed with my mother's oldest sister, Aunt Eva while they were gone. Aunt Eva lived way out in the country. She didn't have any sidewalks or stores where they could go to buy cigarettes. I was glad we didn't live there. Their house was a small wooden place with a kitchen without running water and two small bedrooms and an outhouse. I never knew what an outhouse was until my mother got married! And flies, boy did they have flies, they were in the house in the yard, but mostly in the outhouse. It was the first time in my life I remembered hearing flies making buzzing sounds louder than we talked. They had six children, but Arty and I considered them to have a small family. We said they had a small family because their house was small.

The bedrooms had mattresses on the floor and one dresser. We mostly stayed outside of the house as there was nothing to do in it. On Saturday evenings, everyone in the family had to take a bath. The bathing troth was on the side of the house where it was private. It was filled water with ice cold water from the water pump in the front yard. A bar of yellow soap was thrown into the water. Youngest to oldest, that was the order in which we bathed. Needless to say Arty went first, then me, then the next six. The water never got changed. The good thing was we all had nice clean towels.

In-between the bathing of Bill and Bob, Roberta came running out of the front door screaming, because Bill was trying to throw a snake at her. I saw the long fat black snake and it scared me too. Aunt Eva was sitting in a rocking chair on the dirt knitting. When she heard Roberta scream, she took a pair of scissors threw them at her and stabbed her in the back with them. They stuck in her back! Roberta was screaming, "Pull them out, pull them out." There was blood dripping down her back and without missing a stitch, Aunt Eva hollered, "There, that will teach you not to scream." Arty and I were scared to death. We slept together that night on a mattress on the floor shivering, not from the cold bath, but from fear. Arty and I prayed we wouldn't get stabbed. We had to stay there for four more fearful days. I told Arty, "We are here because Norman took Mommy away." Arty said, "Well he better bring her back." He did. It is the only time I remember us having a baby-sitter.

In the beginning, the marriage seemed good. Good especially for my mother as she was now getting out of bed and taking better care of herself, feeding us, bathing us and doing the laundry. Norman had a car and on Sundays we would go for rides and get ice-cream at the local dairy stand. Arty was not getting beat as much, our mother was not yelling and swearing and we were happy.

## Chapter Nine

# MARTIN STREET

MARTIN ST. WAS WHERE THE FITZGERALD FAMILY lived and now we were moving in. It was considered a better, "neighborhood" than Autumn Ave. The house was very, very small. One bedroom downstairs that was really a dining room and two rooms upstairs at the top of the tiny spiral staircase. Norman's mother lived there alone. Her husband died from a heart attack two months before Norman married our mother.

I think she was excited about us joining her family, but she had many, many rules to follow. She also had a long leather strap hanging on a hook in the kitchen. She said, "Behave or I will hit you with the strap, just as I use to hit Norman with it." Well I don't know if Arty and I can follow rules, we never had them before. My mother told us, "Just do what you need to and keep the old lady quiet." They never got along.

Mrs. Fitzgerald, wanted us to call her just that, "Mrs. Fitzgerald." We wanted to call her Mrs. F., but Mom said we couldn't call her that. Fitzgerald was a long name to say every time you wanted to talk to her, and now that we were living with her, it will take us forever to say her name. She was a small woman with a wickedly short Irish temper and a mean spirited tongue. My mother also called her Mrs. Fitzgerald. Funny a daughter- in -law, would refer to her mother- in- law, by her sur name.

Her house had been built by her late husband in 1901. Like I said it was very small and crooked. It seemed like the house was leaning to one side or the other. The largest window in the house was 12x12 inches. The bathroom had a partial dirt floor and the grass would grow under the tub in the summer time. I once witnessed the cat eating the grass on the side of the tub while I was taking a bath.

We turned the living room into a bedroom for the three of us, because Mom was going to have a baby in November. Arty and I had a set of bunkbeds and we thought that was fun and we got to sleep by ourselves. Arty slept on the top bunk. He hit his head every time he got in or out of his bed. He said it was okay because he was used to getting hit. There was a crib in the corner for the new baby. The crib had pretty yellow blankets and sheets. Our beds had bedbugs and fleas. You could see them, you could smell them and we were covered with bites from head to toe. "Mom the bug bites hurt me and they are itchy." She told me not to, "Scratch too hard." Arty never mentioned his bedbugs, but he too was full of bites.

There was only one small closet in the house and that housed our coats. At Christmas time Arty and I went looking for the hidden presents before the big day. There weren't many places we could look because the house was so tiny, so of course we looked under my mother's bed. Bingo! There they were four bags filled to the top with beautiful shiny Christmas gifts. We carefully looked through each bag being careful not to make too much noise. There were all kinds of goodies, ribbon candy, socks and PJ's for Arty and me, and underwear for both of us. That was good, but where were the toys? Then finally in the last bag far in the corner there it was, the hard to reach pot of gold. In that bag was a truck for Arty and an electric toy oven for me, the kind you use a lightbulb to bake with. We were so happy. Arty played with his truck while I unwrapped the package of frosting that came with the bake set. I ate the frosting and tried to put the cellophane back on the box, but it didn't work. We didn't get caught, 'till wrapping time. Mom didn't say too much about it. On Christmas morning after I opened it she said, "We have to get more icing." We never did.

The kitchen was literally built on the dirt of the back yard. Depending on where you were standing, everything tilted to the left or right,

The dining room had to be turned into the living room, dining area because we had overtaken the tiny house. There was no place in that room to watch TV except by the front door. The only plug was by the front door. Mrs. Fitzgerald didn't own a television, but Norman bought one when we moved in. The TV was a 14 inch black and white with rabbit ears. The room had to be dark, otherwise you couldn't see the picture. So Arty and I sat on the cold damp floor and watched television. We watched, The Lone Ranger, Howdy Doody and Father Knows Best. Mom watched from the kitchen chair with her legs crossed and swinging. She smoked cigarettes and drank coffee. Mrs. Fitzgerald stayed upstairs. My mother told us to never go upstairs, it was the "forbidden place." She didn't socialize with us nor did she ever eat with us. She had a hot plate and a small refrigerator. She came down every morning, emptied her chamber pot, put it on her steps and then went off to

Mass at St. Matthew's Church. It was quite a walk for her, but until she got older, she made the journey every day of the week. She usually came home with two or three things to eat, but never for us. She would take her chamber pot, along with her tid-bits, back up the steps and stay there for the rest of the day, in silence. No TV, no radio.

Arty and I would sneak up at least once a week to check out Mrs. Fitzgerald's place. Her front room at the top of the stairs had a telephone seat. The rest of the room was housed with a small table and two chairs, a small counter and refrigerator. Her back room had a single bed, a nightstand with a lamp on it and a dresser with Catholic statues and lit candles. The back room also had a very small closet. It was so small Arty could hardly fit into it. The ceilings slanted on both sides and I could not stand under it. It was very neat.

On one of the walls in our front room there was a very large picture of Abraham Lincoln. It probably was a lithograph. The eyes on "Ole Abe" seemed to follow you wherever you were in the room. If we were watching TV, so was Abe. He looked at us when we were eating and his eyes followed us if we were leaving the house. Arty and I used to talk to the picture, asking, "How are you today Mr. President?" Luckily he never answered. I wonder what ever happened to the picture of "Ole Abe."

In my mother's tiny bedroom there was a small desk and chair. The desk had two drawers in it. I would sit at the desk and play school. Of course I always was the teacher. I made an attendance record from all of my maternal cousin's names, in all I had over forty students. I would scour the house for any extra pencils or paper we had and once I hit the jackpot and found an old stapler that still had staples in it. I was in heaven. I wrote on the walls with chalk because it rinsed off easily. Miss Emmajoy Regan was very happy in her classroom and in my mind we went on a field trip every day.

Next door to Mrs. Fitzgerald lived her sister-in-law in a big two family house. It had fourteen rooms counting the upstairs apartment. Her name was Aunt Kathleen and her husband was Uncle Shelby. They were wonderful people and their house wasn't crooked and it even had a proper basement. I knew Norman's father didn't build that one.

They had been married for more than thirty years, but never had any children, but they did have sixteen cats, and except for the smell of the fresh ground liver she fed to her cats every day, you would never have known an animal lived there.

Aunt Kathleen immediately took us under her wing when her nephew Norman married my mother. She bought Arty and me nice clothing. She would often stop at the bakery on her way home from work and get us a fancy cookie or cake. She would let us bathe in her big clean bathroom and always give us each a clean washcloth and a towel. She took me to diners and restaurants. They even took Arty and me on the bus to New York City to see the circus. Arty and I were living the good life with Aunt Kathleen and Uncle Shelby.

It was at the circus, we knew Aunt Kathleen was sick because she fainted while she was eating her popcorn. Arty said, "She must really be dying, because nobody would go to sleep if they had popcorn," I agreed. We were able to make it home, but she was never the same as she was plagued with medical problems. She died a few years later. I was angry with my mother, because she wouldn't let me go to the funeral. I had seen dead people before and I wasn't afraid, but my mother said to me, in her kindest voice, "I just want you to remember her how she was." I got to know Aunt Kathleen for four wonderful years. I loved her. She taught me how to act and eat like a lady.

A few weeks before she died, I went to see her and her house was a mess. I knew she didn't like it that way, so I cleaned it for her and then I made fried pork chops with mashed potatoes for her and Uncle Shelby. Shelby and I ate, but she didn't. With her sweet soft voice and pale, frail body, she smiled and said, "Thank you Emmajoy." I never saw her again. When she died she left me all of her jewelry. It was the only inheritance I ever had.

If my mother raised her voice for any reason, Mrs. Fitzgerald would shout to Norman, "Keep that heathen quiet." I didn't know what a heathen was, but I didn't want my mother to be called one. One day I finally asked Mrs. Fitzgerald what a heathen was and she shouted, "It's a Protestant." I said, "Oh," but I didn't know what that meant either. She told me, Arty and I were okay though, because we were baptized Catholic.

Oh boy, I will have to pray for my mother. Mrs. Fitzgerald doesn't like her because she wasn't baptized Catholic and now it's too late because only babies get baptized.

Ironically enough, it was my mother who prayed with me every night for as far back as I can remember. We prayed the "Now I lay me down to sleep," prayer. It was she, who sang and told me about Jesus. So there! My mother wasn't a Protestant nor a heathen because she knew about Jesus.

When my mother was growing up, the family church was, The Salvation Army. Mrs. Fitzgerald, blew a gasket when she heard about that. "And I suppose you sang on the street corners," she said,

"Yes I did." That made me giggle. I was told by Mrs. Fitzgerald to, "Be quiet, because if you don't listen to me, you will turn out just like your mother."

When I visited my father on Sundays, we would go to mass, but when I was on Autumn Ave., I always went to the Salvation Army with my Grandmother, Joy and when I was with Norman, he took me to St. Matthews. I only liked the Salvation Army. I was only a babe myself, but I knew who Jesus was and I knew how to pray.

In late November Harriet and Norman had their first son. They named him Andrew Maynard Fitzgerald. He was a cute chubby baby with a sweet temperament. But Mom was back in bed. Mrs. Fitzgerald would often yell down to let us know the baby was crying as if we couldn't hear him. "Sweet Nelly, Harriet, stop that baby from crying." I would go to my mother's bed and shake her, "Mom get up. The baby is hungry." She replied, "I know he is, give him a bottle." I fixed him a bottle of warm water with evaporated milk and two teaspoons of sugar. And so it began. I was becoming a yet "older soul" and now had to take care of this three month old baby and Mom was pregnant again. I was seven years old.

Mrs. Fitzgerald was furious when she found out my mother was pregnant and made us move out. We moved back home; back to Autumn Ave. There was more room for us there now, as the last of the sisters had married and moved out and two of the other married siblings bought their own homes. The move turned out to be a good thing for Mom as it got her out of bed. She spent a lot of time downstairs with Edna playing cards and drinking coffee.

When we moved back to Autumn Ave., Mom put our bunkbeds along with the mattress on the curb for trash pickup.

## Chapter Ten

# RATS

I WAS SO HAPPY TO LEAVE MARTIN ST. AND THAT school district. I was going home! I would go back to my old school and see my friends and I could walk to the ferry to see my father. At Mrs. Fitzgerald's house, I had to take a taxi to the ferry as it was too far to walk and Norman always complained about the twenty-five cent cost. I could go to Sunday school at The Salvation Army with Nanna Joy. I also went with her to the Friday night ladies' meeting. It was there I could look through the donated clothing and find something clean and intact for Arty and me to wear. We were growing and most of our sparse clothing and shoes only fit us for a couple of months at a time. There was no limit as to what we could take, but I was never greedy. Every once in a while I would find a nice, young girls purse. Pure joy!

So we moved all our belongings into the third floor on Autumn Ave. We now had a spacious kitchen, dining room and living room, and we had a couch and chairs to sit on. Good-bye floors! Shortly after the move, Mom had our new baby, another brother. Her second son from her marriage to, Norman. The first boy would be one year old in two weeks. We were busy. Harriet, had four children. She was twenty-three years old.

When I returned to my old Autumn Ave., school, one of my teachers said, "Why on earth did you ever move back here?" Even though I was just a young child, I knew it was not a good thing and her question stung me. I was so happy to be back until she asked that and that's when I found "shame," and understood what the class system was, even though it wasn't supposed to exist in America. The neighborhood was changing, businesses were closing and many families were moving to the suburbs, where there were fancy new houses. I was ashamed to be back because her words made me feel as if I had done something wrong. I felt as if I didn't belong. She had shamed me.

If I took the word "Shame," wrote it on a piece of paper and carried it around with me for one year, I might never have felt its weight. Yet when spoken, it put a heaviness in my soul. It caused pain in my neck and shoulders and it gave me a bellyache.

We had been back on Autumn Ave., for a while, and I was taking a bath. I was taking my time as Mom was downstairs with Aunt Edna and she took the baby with her. I was singing in the tub, rolling around and enjoying the warm water. It seemed as if those old claw footed tubs were enormous.

All of a sudden, I head a squeaking scratching noise from under the tub. I looked over the side and I saw a very large rat! I screamed and screamed and it sat on the floor and watched me while it was eating something with its paws, like squirrels do! Arty came to my rescue and put a large sauce pot on top of the rat and tried to bang it to death with the noise. It worked. I didn't stick around to see the dead rat, but by now my mother was upstairs to see what all the ruckus was about and assured me the rat was dead. Arty told me that she threw the rat out of the third floor window. Mom took the sauce pan to the sink filled it with water and put it on the stove and started to boil water in it for our spaghetti dinner. "Mom you didn't even wash the pan out that had the R A T in it. Please just throw it away." She told me, "You are always old and picky." I didn't eat that night.

After that I was afraid of the house. I was afraid of the bathroom, the dark hallways and the fourth floor bedrooms. I pounded my feet and clapped my hands everywhere I went. Mom told me the noise would scare the rats away. Well it didn't scare the one in the bathroom! She told me not to worry because, "That was the sick rat and now it's dead." Well I did worry. When my older male cousins heard of what happened with the rat, they taunted me by saying the rats were going to get me, bite me and chew my ears off while I was sleeping. And if one didn't come to my bed by Tuesday, they would find one and put it under my covers. When I went to bed I rolled myself up in my blanket like one would use shrink wrap. Nothing was going to get under my covers. I wasn't even going to use the bathroom.

But, sure enough, there was a rat in the bedroom climbing on the bed and looking straight at me. I screamed so hard my face ached for days. I ran down the stairs and there was one there also. It seemed they were everywhere in the house, daytime, nighttime, it didn't matter. Every hole that could be found in the house or walls were filled with steel wool. I guess they couldn't chew through it. In the night time, you could hear the rats running and chewing in the walls and ceilings. Rat traps were set about the house, fifteen at a time. At night, they sounded like firecrackers going off as the traps echoed a loud "SNAP" in the hallways. The adults were getting tired of getting up at night and having to empty and reset the traps. The only place we never saw or heard the rats was in my grandmother's apartment. Nanna Joy comforted me and loved me. She helped ease my fear. I slept with her until we moved out of Autumn Ave.

I later learned many of the neighborhood homes had infestation problems because of all the houses and buildings being torn down because of early, Urban Renewal. This renewal process was supposed to take down old decaying building and replace them with more desirable buildings in which businesses and middle to upper class people would be attracted to. However for Avon, it did not work. Every building near the river, decayed or not was torn down and not replaced.

The rats were going anywhere they could because their burrows and nests were disturbed. They could only run up, because if they ran down, they were in the river. I prayed and asked God to send all of the rats in our house away. He did. Within a few months the rats were exterminated and we never saw another one again. In fact we didn't see any cats or squirrels either. The poison was strong; I think it killed off most of the small animals.

I had had many respiratory infections since birth and even had pneumonia twice before I was three. I now had trouble jumping rope, playing hop scotch and joining in the double dutch rounds. Had the strong poison affected me? Nobody wanted me on their team. I always got picked last on the team, because I was ill. I was never good at athletic stuff to begin with, but now I was dead in the water, as my own cousins told me to go home and rest, but horrid fear arouse again. It was the same fear I experienced when I saw the rats. I now had breathing problems even at rest.

I also had a problem with bacterial infections on my skin. I had boils, impetigo and carbuncles. All of these types of skin problems come from being dirty and lack of good hygiene. My mother did take me to the doctor to have the boils lanced, but they often returned. I still have scars from them. "Lord, help me please, I am afraid." Fear was with me everywhere I went. I was even afraid of the inside plumbing of the toilet tank. I was afraid of men wearing work boots. I was afraid of the air raid drills we had in school, on which all of the students were required to squat under their desks and cover their heads with their hands. Fear had gripped me, but I didn't tell a soul.

According to the Bible, 1 John 4:18 states, "There is no fear in love. But perfect love drives out fear, because fear has to do with punishment." NIV.

Those rats were fear alright, straight from the pits of hell. As a child I thought they must be the devil's animals.

Maybe we should have stayed at Mrs. Fitzgerald's. She only had bedbugs and fleas and I wasn't afraid of them. When I tried to tell my mother about my breathing problems and my weak legs, she said, "Have you been smoking my cigarettes?" to which I replied, "No, I did not." She then stated, "Well you had your polio shots, so don't worry about it."

In 2007 my two grand-loves, invited me over to their house to show me something they had gotten from the store. I gladly got into my car, drove to the bakery to pick up some cookies and away I drove, anxious to see what they had gotten. I walked into the house and they were cute as buttons greeting me with their big smiles and giggles. I could see their clothing moving and their giggles got louder. "What, what did you get?" I asked. They both proceeded to dig under their clothing and at the same time they said, "Tada, here hold them." and presented me with two white rats with red ugly eyes. Ugh! "Please put them back in the cage and put their cover over the cage and no, I didn't want to hold them." We sat on the floor and played around and I pretended I was the big rat and tickled them under their clothing. We then ate the cookies. A few short weeks later my daughter called to inform me the rats had babies. They took them back to the store where they had gotten them. The store owner said he would be happy to resell them to someone else. Thank you Jesus.

## Chapter Eleven

# ROACHES

AFTER THE RAT INFESTATION, THE HOUSE WAS plagued with cockroaches. Ugh! They were not as scary as the rats, because they always ran away when the lights came on, but none the less, I didn't like them. They would crawl on you when you didn't know it. They would hide in your shoes, and I would always find them in the kitchen around the sink. One time I found a dead one in a pot of cooked sauce.

The house always smelled of chemicals, even if there was a cake baking, the smell of bug spray overtook the house. I think we had more cans of insect spray than the local hardware store. Every room in our apartment had a can of bug spray in it. One afternoon my mother was ironing some clothing and accidently sprayed Norman's shirt with bug spray instead of starch, when she realized what she had done, she threw the shirt away.

One early morning two of my brothers were in their crib, crying, and waiting to be taken care of. I had gone up to my mother's apartment to get ready for school. I got dressed and the babies continued to cry. They were one and two years old. "Mom, get up the babies are crying. They are hungry." "You take care of them please, better yet stay home from school and take care of them today." I really didn't want to miss school because I was a good student and I was glad to be away from the house. But I stayed home and tended to the babies. I had to first scrub the bottles clean as they were caked with sour milk. The one year old was trying to drink out of his baby bottle, but the poor thing gagged every time he tried. They were screaming so hard I finally put them on the kitchen floor so I could talk to them while I prepared their bottles. I fixed their bottles with warm water, evaporated milk and two teaspoons of sugar.

I then needed to change them, both were soaking wet and so was their crib. They had on cloth diapers and rubber pants. Disposable diapers had not yet been invented. When I changed the first baby, he had the worst diaper rash I had ever seen. He screamed when I wiped him and I started to cry. "Mom, please get out of bed. The babies need help." She didn't budge. I ran downstairs to get Aunt Edna. I was still crying. She was busy with her own family, but came up to help me anyway. She brought diaper cream with her. She changed and soothed the bottoms of my baby brothers, cleaned the crib, gathered the dirty diapers and sheets and took them down-stairs to launder them. She left me the cream, but before she left, she kicked the pullout sleeper sofa my mother was asleep on and through her gritted teeth yelled, "Harriet get up." But Harriet didn't.

I put the babies in their high chairs and the "old sister/mother soul" went to work. I cleaned the kitchen, and gave the babies some cereal. I then played with them for a while, and then put them down for a nap. I did some laundry with the wringer washing machine that was stored in the corner of the kitchen. I then hung the clothes up on the line to dry. The clothesline was very long, almost fifty feet. I only did one load because I hated sitting on the ledge of the third floor window to hang the clothes out to dry. I made sure I had washed some of my own clothes and I washed a shirt and a pair of trousers for Arty.

By now the babies were awake, and I had bottles ready for them and I was also going to give them each a jar of fruit. Mom was still asleep.

I walked into their tiny closet bedroom and saw a brown circle on the wall. The two year old baby was squirting his bottle on the wall and when he did, they both giggled, "What are you two up to?" I smiled. The younger baby then reached through the crib bars, into the circle with his cute little hand and grabbed a handful of cockroaches and put it in his mouth! The circle was a circle of roaches! I screamed, scared the babies and they started to cry, but my scream woke up my mother. I yanked them both from the crib, cleaned out the mouth of the one who was trying to eat the cock-roaches and put them in their highchairs.

When I told Mom what happened, and she said, "Well go spray the wall." The roaches were still there in a circle, because they were eating the milk from the bottle that had been squirted on the wall. I sprayed the wall with the bug spray and some of the roaches died, but most of them scattered away. I swept up the dead bugs with a broom and put them in the garbage can in the kitchen. Mom went into the kitchen to make coffee. I was eight years old and Mom was pregnant again. She sat at the table with her legs crossed and swinging, smoking her cigarette.

The bugs seemed to multiply weekly, but no one except me seemed to be concerned about our thousand or so roaches. Norman, eventually invested in bug bombs, the kind you set off, but are so toxic you have to leave the house. So one bright sunny Sunday afternoon, Norman decided he was going to set off the bug bombs and we would go for a ride and get some ice-cream. By now our family had grown by one more baby. This time a sister. We hurried to get ready and we watched Norman, as he set off the bug bomb. The bomb made a hissing noise and it made a straight line cloud as if all of its contents were coming out at once.

We left the apartment, marched down the stairs and all piled into the car. No seat belts no car seats. I held one toddler on my lap, my mother held the youngest baby in the front seat on her lap and Arty and I had a toddler sitting between us in the back seat. As we are ready to pull away from the curb my mother realized she forgot a hat for our baby sister and told me to, "Run upstairs and get a bonnet for the baby, you know the pretty white one." I handed our brother to Arty, ran into the house, up the stairs, opened the apartment door and immediately screamed. There were dozens of dead cockroaches falling from the ceiling. They were falling on my head and shoulders. They made a sort of clicking, typing sound as they hit the floor and I could barely see or breathe. I got back into the car coughing and crying. I told my mother, "There are dead roaches falling from the ceiling, and falling on me and I couldn't see or breath," and she said, "That's what supposed to happen when you set off the bombs." Arty picked a couple of dead cockroaches out of my hair. I never did get the bonnet. My mother told me I was always "screaming." Norman pulled the car away from the curb with one hand, with the other he was holding his whiskey. I never screamed in the house again.

When we came back from our four hour ride, I refused to go into the apartment until I knew the roaches had been picked up.

Mom swept them up and Arty gave me the all clear sign. It's a wonder any of us survived.

Those roaches were everywhere in the house except in Nanna Joy's apartment. I know that apartment was a safe area set aside by God for me. The apartment is where I found peace and safety.

When I was in the third grade, I always wanted to invite Mrs. Johnson, my favorite teacher to dinner, but I never did, because I was afraid she would see a bug on the table while we were eating. Mrs. Johnson died as Aunt Kathleen died; cancer. The word nobody said out loud. When cancer was talked about they would whisper and say, "Cancer," or refer to it as the big C.

It was during this time I started to feel my life was a "Burden." I became withdrawn and short tempered with the babies. I was mad at my mother. My, "old soul" was crying out. I wanted to be taken care of. I wanted the beatings to stop. Frequently my baby brother would bang his head against the wall after my mother beat him with a shoe for soiling his diaper. He was two and a half! I wanted Arty to be clean and have something to eat. I think I loved her children more than she did.

Why was my name Emmajoy? I was Emmasad. I hated my name... Joy, nope, I should have been called, Sorry Emma. I was sorry I was ever born into this family. I wanted my mother and father together. I wanted to live in a big house without rats or bugs. I wanted cake on Tuesdays. And I wanted nice clothing and hair. I didn't want to do laundry, or cook, or mop floors. I wanted to go to school and not change dirty baby diapers. I was supposed to be a kid, play hop-scotch, and eat honeysuckles and let ice cream make my face sticky and dirty.

But I was burdened. I didn't know what to call it back then, but what a burden life was for me. Burden is a terrible, disastrous place to be. It lies to you and makes you keep commitments to life in an improper order. Burden does not care how old or young you are, it's just a, "Burden." Burden told me if I didn't get up early, do the laundry, feed the babies and clean the house, I wasn't doing my job. Burden took my name, Emmajoy. I was now just, Emma.

I was eight years old, taking care of Mom's chores, and three boys. I want to go to school with pretty hair and a nice clean dress and underwear. My mother always said, "Make sure your underwear is clean." Really, she knows she didn't do the laundry!

## Chapter Twelve

# ROAMING HANDS

SINCE I WAS TWENTY YEARS OLD I HAVE THOUGHT about "roaming hands." What are they really? I realize roaming hands is a play on words that is usually referring to something sexual in nature, but I believe, "roaming hands" can be described as, hands that are about a business they should not be involved in; thus roaming hands. Unfortunately I have known both definitions of them.

My first remembrance of someone touching me, was an adult male. He was an in-law in the family. He asked me to sit on his lap while we were watching television. The room was dark and he was sitting in a rocking chair in the corner. I was glad to sit on his lap and not the hard floor. When I climbed onto his lap I thought I felt something strange, but, I didn't know what was going on, I was five years old. His hands were busy with himself and he was using me as a shield to cover up. I thought he had ants in his pants because he couldn't sit still. I actually climbed off his lap and he told me to, "Get back here." I didn't. That was the only time he ever bothered me. I was five years old.

At age seven I saw what a full grown naked man looked like. I was innocently lying on my mother's pull out sleeper sofa after my bath in my line dried fresh pajamas. The baby was sleeping, Arty was on the fourth floor sleeping and Mom was downstairs playing cards with Aunt Edna. I was going to watch a TV show then go down to Nanna Joy's apartment and go to sleep.

When I saw him, I immediately turned onto my stomach and pretended to just watch TV. He got closer and closer to me. I could feel him breathing, I could smell the cigarettes and beer on his breath. He removed the bottom half of my PJ's and the roaming hands were all over me.

My heart was pounding, my breathing was nearly stopped because now, I was now pretending I was dead. *WHERE IS MY MOTHER? I NEED HER!* But she didn't come upstairs, in fact I could hear her downstairs laughing. Well the beer man was finally off of me. He rolled me over and said, "By the way there is no such thing as Santa Clause and if you tell anybody I was here I will kill your brothers." I don't remember the rest of the evening.

I now hated Autumn Ave., and asked God to burn it down. I do remember the following days and weeks and never went into my mother's apartment after supper again.

I found roaming hands in other people's houses too! My girl-friend's brother, an old stinky neighbor, and even an Aunts house. None of them were able to hurt me as the beer man did, because I didn't stick around long enough. As soon as they got the demon look in their eye and touched my leg, despite my breathing problems, I became a sprint runner and ran as fast as I could to any outside door.

I never told anyone of these accounts. No one would believe me anyway because I was the ugly, dirty kid from Autumn Ave. I wanted these men, "put in jail." I wanted the cops to come and take them away. I wanted to tell my father what happened, but it wasn't his weekend. In my very young soul, "Anger" spoke to me and told me not to worry, because, "I'm so mad nothing like this is ever going to happen to me again." Well it did. "Shame" told me to be quiet because maybe this is my fault. There was a spiritual battle going on and it seemed all the demons from hell were winning.

No other abuse occurred in that house because I never left Nanna Joys side, but then we moved.

One cold dark night in the small house where I made Arty brush his teeth with dirty dish water, the beer man appeared again.

I was sleeping in my bedroom and I smelled that awful smell again. He was here. He went into the front room, took off his clothing and went down to the bathroom. While he was in the bathroom I searched his trousers and took a dollar so I could take the public bus to school in the AM and perhaps buy a hot lunch at school. I never stole, but that night I was taking the beer man's dollar. The only children who took buses to school for free were the ones who lived in the country. It was wintertime and the walk to school was nearly a mile and I was always freezing when I arrived. I didn't have snow pants or leggings and I was only allowed to wear a skirt or dresses to school.

He eventually climbed onto my bed. He was drunk and weak. He was angry because he realized I took a dollar from his trousers. I don't know how he knew, but he did. Maybe I wasn't a good thief.

He started to smother me with his own face, announced what he was going to sexually do to me and then kill me for taking his dollar.

He then tried to force himself on me, but I fought back. When that didn't work he tried to smother me with my pillow. I yelled for him to stop and pushed him with all of my might off of me. He made a loud thud noise when he hit the floor and he stayed there for a few hours. I didn't get up, I just stayed in bed wide awake waiting for my mother to come to my rescue. She was in the next wide-opened door room. She never got out of bed, but she could see my bed from hers.

Eventually, I fell asleep and when I woke up the beer man was gone from my room. He never touched me again. Arty told me he could hear "something" was going on in my room, but for the fear of getting beat, stayed in his own room with our other brothers.

Again, I told no one about the abuse. If my father and uncles knew, I think they would have killed him. But the "beer man" was taking a huge toll on my young mind, and I became mean and I started to hate my mother. I begged God to put me with another family, like the one on Father Knows Best. Well, we moved, but I did not go to another family.

I have heard many stories of incest and abuse in my family. It breaks my heart to think of such vile acts, but I can't dwell on them for they could devour me.

But there are roaming hands everywhere. Mom's hands were roaming when she beat Arty. Norman's hands were roaming when he was drinking his whiskey. Neil's hands were roaming when he worked at the bar. My hands were roaming when I stole the beer man's dollar. Roaming hands are never good.

*Chapter Thirteen*

# BACK TO MARTIN STREET

---

AFTER AUNT KATHLEEN DIED, NORMAN FOUND out he was the heir of her estate and we moved into her beautiful house on Martin Street. It was a two lot property. The first lot was a nice long wide driveway and the second lot was, of course the house. There we were, right next door to good old Mrs. Fitzgerald. Norman, his heathen wife and all their kids, on Martin Street. I hoped this would have solved all of our problems, but of course it did not. In fact, things started to sink even deeper into darkness.

Mom was going to have another baby, this would be child number four for the Fitzgerald's and as a family it would boost our number to eight.

The house was fully furnished with beautiful antiques, beds, tables, chairs, lamps, linens, dishes and appliances. Everything was there we could have ever needed or wanted. Uncle Shelby was still alive, so he moved upstairs where there was a private bed and bathroom separate from the apartment. All of Aunt Kathleen's cats had been euthanized at her request upon her death.

My mother hated all of the antiques in the house and one by one moved them to the curb for the trash man to pick up. We kept the beds, dressers and living room furniture, but not the lamps or end tables. The dining room table got sold to a neighbor who had an antique store, and he showed up to buy it while we were eating our supper, so we all had to remove our plates, so he could take the table. So there we were five of us gathered around in a circle of chairs finishing our meal. I also think the neighbor took most of what Mom put out to the curb as trash. After we finished eating, we put the kitchen table in the dining room and put the leaf in it so we could all fit at the table. The kitchen still had a small table in it, enough to seat four people.

We moved from our small house to the big one in the fall, so Arty and I had to go to yet another school. We were not warmly welcomed there. The students AND teachers were bullying Arty because of his unkempt scrawny body. They were also making fun of me because of my dirty tattered appearance. I now felt angrier than ever. Now I knew how Arty felt, and it wasn't good. He was in the fourth grade and I was in the sixth. If Aunt Kathleen was alive we wouldn't look like this, she would have given us nice clothing, haircuts and shoes. And we would have lunch money! All of the children were from a mostly upper middle class, and then there was Arty and Emma. I never told anyone what my middle name was.

Practically every student in that school bought a hot meal at lunchtime. The whole school had lunch at the same time. The younger children were served first and we lined up according to grade. Lunch was twenty five cents for a hot meal and fifteen cents for a cold sandwich and that included one pint of ice cold milk. If we only bought a milk, it was five cents. Arty and I would share a pint of milk. We weren't supposed to sit together at lunch, but we did.

Needless to say Arty and I brought what we could scrape together for lunch at home, but it never amounted to much. Sometimes it was just two or three piece of bread. We were so ashamed, and sometimes we only had our bread in wax paper, without the brown paper bag.

The teasing was relentless, "What's the matter kid, did your "poor" family forget your food." "You don't belong here. Go back to where you came from." Those words stung the same way as the teacher who asked why I was moving back down to the Autumn Ave., school. We didn't fit in, we were never going to fit in this upper class neighborhood. After all we were just the kids from Autumn Ave.

One cold foggy morning it was pouring out, and of course I didn't have a rain coat, so I wore a big heavy sweater. I did have an umbrella but it didn't keep me all that dry as the wind kept blowing the rain. My sweater got wet and heavy and made me cold. Arty was cold too. He didn't have an umbrella or a sweater. When we got to school we saw other students being dropped off by their parents, or by taxies.... if only.

My feet were also cold and a little wet, but not too bad. I had on two different colored penny loafers, one black and one brown. I tried to polish the brown one black, but it didn't work out too well. I chose to wear them that day to try and help keep my feet dry. You see both the brown and black pair of loafers had a hole in the bottom of the shoes, but if I wore one of each color, I had a pair without a hole.

The whole class laughed at me when the sixth grade teacher pointed out I had two different color shoes on. She said out loud, "Are you color blind, or did you make a mistake with your choices this morning." No on both accounts. I went home that day, put a big piece of cardboard in the bottom of the black loafers, and threw the brown pair away. That same teacher got at least one "dig" in me every day. She always had a nasty comment to make about my clothing, shoes or hair.

Then I went to Nanny Joy's house and took a pair of her shoes, (as I was nearly her size) and wore them to school for the rest of the year. When Nanny Joy saw me wearing the shoes she smiled and said, "I wondered what happened to those shoes. "I'm glad they found a good home." I also took a couple of skirts, and a few pair of underwear along with a couple of safety pins to hold the underwear up. I cut the skirts off a few inches and hemmed them. They were old lady fashionable, but I didn't care. They weren't smelly or ripped.

Even when I would get 100's on my homework and tests, this same mean spirited teacher would say, "Well I don't know how you did it, but here it is," while she was snapping my papers at me.

Son number three and child number four was born to Mom and Norman, on St. Patrick's Day. He was so cute and perfect, he became my favorite. I missed a lot of school helping my mother take care of her family, but that was now okay with me because of the teacher and those rotten kids. Mom was glad to write me an absent note for school, because it meant she could stay in bed. I soon learned how to copy her handwriting and forge her name, and then wrote my own notes.

I now had a whole house to clean and of course Mom was back in bed. The children were pretty good as they usually listened to me. They didn't consider me a child, they referred to me, "As one of them," meaning an adult. I was nearly eleven years old.

I no longer played or hung out with any of my cousins, instead I drank coffee and played cards with the adult Aunts and Uncles every Sunday at Aunt Edna's house. I could play poker with the best of them, and I was the only child-cousin allowed to play.

But I did miss my cousin, Faith. She was my soul-mate, best friend. She lived clear across the other side of town. When I lived on Autumn Ave., I would walk to her house and if I was allowed, I would stay all day. She was a beautiful girl with dark brown curly hair, hazel eyes and a smile that caused you to wear sunglasses. People often mistook us for sisters, as there was a strong family resemblance. I loved Faith, she let me be myself, happy or sad, she stuck by me. She had an older brother, but we didn't bother with him too much.

I was often mean to Faith and would say hurtful things because of jealousy, but she never once turned away from the bond we had. She had a kind gentle voice that could sooth your soul. She was gracious and even as a child she acted like a lady.

When I was with Faith, she took care of me! She helped me find things to wear, and would help me fix my hair. She always made sure I had something to eat. We went to Sunday school together at The Salvation Army and played our tambourines. We were Sunbeams together and worked hard to earn our merit badges. We went for two weeks each summer to camp, together, in upstate New York. She taught me how to ride a bike.

Her mother was my mother's sister. Her name was Ruth. Aunt Ruth loved me. She would often let me tag-a-long with her family to the local swimming beach. She packed the best lunches and always made sure I had a drink, a towel and a bathing suit. Ruth was an avid bowler and golfer. She was a pioneer woman in our family.

She was a hard working single mother with two children, who managed to make her own life after she moved away from Autumn Ave. She was one of the first sisters in my mother's family to learn how to drive. That might sound trivial, but back in her day, it was a big thing. My mother had eight sisters, but, only two of them drove.

It's really ironic the relationship Faith and I had, because (my mother) Harriet, really only related to, Edna and did not care for her other sisters, especially Ruth. I once heard my favorite Aunt-in-law talk about my mother and she stated, "It was difficult to predict what Harriet would do." It was true. Mom was friendly, but you never knew what mood she was going to be in.

So when we moved back to Martin Street, and my time with Faith became less and less until we were both leading our own lives, and not seeing one another for years at a time, but that didn't affect our relationship. We still loved each other.

Norman lost his job, because the construction company moved its headquarters to another city. There wasn't much need for construction in Avon. Urban Renewal continued tearing everything down and the working force industries of the city were moving out too. He was able to find a job in a local bakery, but I don't think he made much money. But they did have income from the house because it had an upstairs apartment, and they had the child support money from my father, but we already know Norman did not handle money wisely.

Soon after Norman went to work for the bakery, he stopped coming home in the evenings. Instead, he was visiting the local bars, running up big tabs and drinking whiskey.

Most of our food came from a small grocery store at the end of our block. We never had much, but most of what we did have, came from, "Martin's Market." Norman had made an arrangement for us to be able to go to the local grocery store anytime we needed something and put it on a tab. It sounded very good to us, especially because Norman no longer had a car. He claimed he could no longer afford the insurance, but Mrs. Fitzgerald told me he lost the car in a poker game, because the guy he lost it to asked her if she wanted to buy it back because the insurance was in her name. My Uncle would take my mother to the big grocery store once every five weeks or so and she would get some things there. We also had other generous family members and neighbors who knew we had many mouths to feed. At our house, toilet paper, tooth paste and personal hygiene items were always in demand but hard to come by.

Every day after school, either Arty or I would go to Martins Market and get supper, which mostly consisted of a loaf of sliced white bread, a gallon of milk and eight slices of bologna. Every two days we would get a box of cereal. On the first of the month, we would also get eight slices of cheese, but that was usually only once a month. We absolutely could not have even an extra glass of milk or there would be no cereal in the morning. Soon we were being denied our purchases at Martin's Market because Norman was not paying the bills. UGH! The store clerk would say to me, "Go tell Norman to pay the bill and you can have what you want." I would relay the message to my mother and it usually took a few days for it to be resolved.

"Emmajoy, go to the bar and knock on the window until someone sees you and when they come to the door, ask them to get, Norman Fitzgerald for you, and tell him you need a dollar. I need cigarettes, bread and milk." "Really, really Mom, you want me to go to the bar and knock on the window?" "Yes, I need cigarettes. Now go." Off I went to the corner, just a few houses from ours and I knock on the window, but the window was a little high, so I couldn't see in. Finally someone came to the door and I shouted, "Is Norman Fitzgerald in there?" "Yes, he's here." A male voice piped back. We knew the bar was now his new home. Norman came to the door and I gave him the message from Mom, and he grudgingly gave me the dollar. I crossed the street, went into Martin's Market and made my purchase. I then went home and gave Mom her cigarettes and put the bread and milk away. Well that wasn't as bad as I thought it would be, but I didn't like going to the bar. I told Arty, "I went to the bar and asked Norman for some money so we could get some food from Martins and he gave me a dollar." Arty replied, "Wow, can I go with you next time?" I told him, "I will think about it, But I don't ever want to go again." But I did have to go again and again After a while Norman went to several bars in a day, so I often would have to walk to all of his favorite places, knock on the window and try and find him, because Mom always needed a dollar. After a while I grew tall enough and I could look into the windows of the local taverns and Norman would come outside when he saw me.

Norman's drinking was completely out of control and he had lost his job at the bakery. He went to the bars every morning around nine AM and stayed until they threw him out. Usually around ten or eleven PM. We didn't care, the less we saw of him the better. He would usually fall into a drunken sleep about fifteen minutes after he came home, but if he stayed awake, there was always trouble.

Norman got into the habit of waking us kids up around ten PM two or three nights a week and lining us up according to height. Of course I was first, because I was the tallest. He was so drunk he could hardly sit upright in a chair. We were all in our underwear and he would ask in a loud slurry deep voice, "Who is the king?" We didn't know who the king was. We knew who the president was, but we didn't know who the king was. He would scream out, "I am the king, now bow down to me." The little guys didn't even know what bow down meant. Again he screamed for us to bow down to him. Arty bowed down, and elbowed the rest of our brothers to do the same and they did. He then banged our heads together, kicked, slapped and punched us. I did not bow down to him, I went back into my bedroom, moved the dresser in front of the door and I was never going to let Norman wake me up or hit me again. I was "ANGRY." This behavior lasted for a few years until his sons were big enough and tired enough to stop Norman's abuse. They would not line up nor bow or answer his questions. Shortly after Uncle Shelby died and my Mom moved me into the private bed and bath upstairs away from the rest of the family. I loved it. I knew it was her way of protecting me.

In one of these early these line-ups, Norman told us he had a dog when he was a little boy who died because he sniffed another dog's poop. We all laughed and when we did he banged all our heads together for several seconds really hard. Mom stayed in her bedroom supposedly fast asleep. When Norman's third son was three years old he said he was going to grow up, get a gun, and, "Shoot Daddy."

The move back to Martin Street, bought new problems, but it didn't have rats or roaches. But we didn't have a telephone. If we had an important call or needed to make one, we used Mrs. Fitzgerald as a secretary. She was grumpy about it, but she did help us out.

Mrs. Fitzgerald's brother was a Priest in the Catholic Church. If he was visiting her we had to "Bless" ourselves as we passed her house and we were not allowed to talk on her sidewalk. If it was Sunday, we weren't allowed to ride a bike or play outside. Father Joseph seemed like a kind man. Every time he came to visit, he would stand outside until he saw the six of us, and he would then say a prayer for us and sprinkle us with Holy Water. He would then give us each a piece of candy. One year he was visiting on Ash Wednesday and we had our own private altar in Mrs. Fitzgerald's house on which we all received our ashes, but of course no candy, because it was lent.

When Norman lost his car in the poker game, we started to go to St. John's Church as St. Matthew's was too far to walk. At first, Norman would take with him anybody who was old enough to walk, except my mother. She never went to Mass. This went on for a few years, and after Mass I would hurry over to the Salvation Army, as I considered that my church and I loved the people and fellowship there. Soon Norman stopped going to church, but insisted I go, but he didn't want me going to the, The Salvation Army. His proof that I went to Mass, was me bringing home the bulletin. So I would run over to St. John's, pick up a bulletin and then go the Salvation Army. That too lasted for about a year, then I didn't pick the bulletin up anymore. When Mrs. Fitzgerald, found out I wasn't going to Mass she called me a "heathen." Norman didn't seem to care.

It was soon to be Christmastime again, and Mom said she wanted to go to Main St., to pick up a few things. I was so happy, Mom and I were going shopping! I had visions of her and me getting dressed up, fixing our hair and walking down Main St., with nice kerchiefs on our heads. Maybe we would go to one of the coffee shops and have lunch or get an ice-cream at the local five & ten.

The next day came, and she got out of bed and told Arty to watch the kids for a while, because we were going shopping. Arty was as shocked as I was. We are ready to leave the house. I fixed myself up a bit but Mom, took a kerchief, wrapped it around her head and tied it in the front, and then put Norman's big, wool, long coat on. She walked faster than I wanted to, and I had a hard time keeping up. I was still having some breathing trouble. We finally reached a store, where she bought some underwear for Arty. I'm so happy I could cry! The woman put the underwear in a small bag, but my mother asked her to put it in a large shopping bag as we had more shopping to do. Cheerfully the woman smiled and gave Mom a very large shopping bag with handles.

"Go look at the pretty dresses and tell me which one you like." Really? Did my mother just tell me go pick out a new dress? I'm in heaven. So I immediately dashed to the dresses. I picked out a simple, but nice dress, and thought to myself, 'I'm going to wear this for Christmas dinner." The Salvation Army always gave us a very large basket of food for Christmas. I returned to where my mother was shopping and I saw her put a ring with my birthstone on it, in the large bag. She didn't pay for it. My happiness left me. I handed Mom the dress, she looked at it said "Okay." I walked away. I knew what she was doing, and now, I'm afraid. She quickly put the dress under her coat, and she said, "Hurry up, we have to go." We walked home very, very fast. But we had to stop on a side street because several items were now falling out of Norman's coat. Mom unloaded her coat, put all of the gifts in the second bag she had, but I have no idea where she got that one from. I carried that bag home. It was heavy. Her voice resonated in my head, "Don't ever steal."

Later that week on Christmas Eve, my mother and I were watching TV when Norman came home earlier than expected. He was, of course, drunk. When my mother heard him fumble with the front door key, she ran to bed and said, "Wait ten minutes and he will go to bed and we will play cards later." We also still had a few things to wrap for the kids, before we went to bed.

Well Norman came into the TV room and asked where my mother was. I lied and told him she had gone to bed earlier. "Well then, I should beat you right now." He picked up her lit cigarette from the ashtray and said, "So this is what you do when nobody is watching." My mother left the room in such a hurry when she heard him coming, she didn't put her cigarette out. Oh great here he goes again, but I told him, to "Be quiet and go to bed." He did, but not before kicking the fully decorated Christmas tree over. An hour later my mother came back into the room. I had finished wrapping the gifts, and I picked up and fixed the tree as best as I could. I went to bed. Some of the boxes were ruined because they got wet from the water in the tree stand.

The next morning, I opened my gifts. They were the dress and ring and couple of other things. I wore the dress, but I threw the ring away.

I now feel like an old lady and I'm twelve. Norman has had a heart attack and can no longer work, but that's okay as he is now getting disability money. So we were slightly better off, but not much.

Mom's wringer washing machine broke and she wasn't replacing it. We now were going to the laundromat and washing and drying all of our clothing on the same day! But we were still often hungry as Norman was now visiting bars even further away than I could walk to, so I couldn't go get the dollar to buy bread and milk, and more often than not, Martin's Market tab was on hold due to lack of payment.

One particular day Mom gave me two dollars to do the wash. We used six washing machines at the cost of twenty five cents each, and then two dryers, at the cost of ten cents each. The dryers were very large and they held at least two loads of clothing, but I always had to put more than a dime in them because they only ran for ten minutes. So we always needed to run the dryers longer to completely dry all of the clothing. I always bought my own soap powder.

One day I was cold and hungry and just overall disgusted, and didn't want to do much, but I had to go to the laundromat. So I filled the very large coach style baby carriage with all of the clothing, pulled up the head cover to the carriage, covered the whole front with a tucked in blanket, as if to protect a baby from the wind and headed up the street. I was glad we had the carriage, because there was no way I could have carried that much laundry. I was walking as fast as I could up the street, because pushing the carriage loaded with dirty clothes was always an embarrassment to me. I stopped at the red light waiting to cross the street and I saw one of my class-mates. She came close to the carriage, and said, "Oh let me see the baby." I said, "No, not today," and angled the carriage away from her, so she couldn't see in, but she followed me as I kept the carriage going in circles. She got the hint I wasn't going to let her see the baby and she left. Whew, that was a close one. When I finally got to the laundromat I was mad that I had to have a baby carriage with clothes in it. The carriage should have had a baby in it, after all we had plenty of them at home. I was so aggravated, I put all of the clothes in two washers. They were so full they barely tumbled. I then went to the local diner and ordered a cheeseburger with fries and a soda. This is my first remembrance of stress eating. I went back to the laundromat, dried and folded the clothes and went home. The carriage stayed at the laundromat the whole time. Back then, no one bothered anyone's baby carriages. In fact women would often go to the store and leave their babies outside on the street while they were shopping. Toddlers were harnessed inside the carriages and sleeping infants were just covered up.

You could tell something wasn't right about that day's laundry, so I never did that again.

## Chapter Fourteen

# REDEMPTION

---

IT'S AN OLD RHETORICAL CLICHÉ QUESTION THAT will never be answered here on earth, and that is, "Why do bad things happen, especially to children?" Is there no God? Well yes there is, and I know Him. He has three parts. He is the Father, He is the Son and He Is the Holy Spirit.

Norman had been admitted to the local Veterans Administration Hospital (VA) for a variety of diseases and problems related to alcohol. He was able to be treated by the VA because he was in the Navy during WWII.

He had been an alcoholic all of his adult life. His prognoses was not good and we were all preparing for his death. He had major serious health issues and one of them was, severe atherosclerosis, and he was in danger of losing his legs. Somehow he was able to recover, but he stayed at the VA as a nursing home patient. He finally had enough whiskey. He was now eighty four years old.

He was there for a year when he took a turn for the worse, and had to be transferred back to the hospital. They were doing all they could for him, but he was not responding. Mom had only been to see him a couple of times since his admission. I offered to drive her to see him, but she didn't want to go.

Mom received a call from the VA one morning to inform the family, "Mr. Fitzgerald was going to be transferred to a larger hospital, because he was going to need surgery." The hospital he was going to was a couple hours away. He was there about a week before they did the surgery, but Mom didn't want to go see him. He was deathly ill.

When Norman had his second heart attack several years before that, Mom didn't go to see him then either. I did. I was thirty-nine years old. I went to visit him in the ICU of our local hospital and I just bluntly gave him the Gospel message in three easy steps. Do you believe in God and the Trinity? Do you believe Jesus died for your sins and He rose again and that you are a sinner? Then ask Him for forgiveness. He said yes to all and then asked Jesus to forgive him! I didn't expect him to respond to the Gospel at all. But he knew the alternative if he didn't. Nobody wants to go to hell. After he quietly repented, my own hardness and hate for him started to melt away. He looked me straight in the eye and said, "You of all people, coming to me at a time like this to make sure I go to heaven." His words have stuck with me since he spoke them. I then left his room. I never went back to visit him, but he recovered and eventually came back home, where he continued to drink his whiskey.

Two thousand and five, was life or death for Norman. If he doesn't have immediate surgery to remove his left leg, the gangrene will kill him. We are summoned to go the hospital, but Mom still refuses to go.

Norman had the surgery and all went well, but he still was is in critical condition. His sons and daughter are with him, but Harriet is not. He had asked his daughter to, *go get his bride*. They give her the message, but she said she was still too busy to go on a two hour one way road trip. But the hospital called Mom two days later and they now need permission to remove the other leg as it is also gangrenous. Without the surgery he will surely die. She gave them a verbal consent over the phone, as Norman was too drugged from the first amputation just a couple of days ago. She said, "Now we should go see him." We piled into the car and headed north. By the time we arrived at the hospital, Norman was out of surgery. He has lost both of his legs, and his prognoses was grave. The whole family is now at the hospital, and we really have come just to say good-bye to Norman as he passes to heaven.

One by one, we entered Norman's room to say good-bye to him. He was too weak to acknowledge our presence. In his room we could only hear the beep, beep, beep of his heart monitor. There were strict orders to "not resuscitate" him if his heart stopped, and this was at his request.

My mother was the last to visit him. I know he was waiting for her. His sons and daughter were all crying, but Mom and I were not. Arty wasn't there as he lived out of state. We stayed at the hospital for several hours, and eventually we all left. Norman died a few hours after we arrived home. A kind nurse called my mother to let her know she was with him, when he died. He was eighty-five years old.

We now had to get Norman back to Avon. I thought we could fit him in the trunk of the car, after all he didn't have any legs, but we knew it was against the law to carry around a dead body. We all had a good laugh about that, because the one thing that was great about our clan was humor. It helped us through many of life's tragedies.

Norman was finally back in Avon, and we had his service at a local funeral home. There were many people there and a few spoke at his eulogy. In particular, one women got up to speak and she introduced herself and said she was a nurse at the VA. She had taken care of Norman for much of his stay at the local VA nursing home. She said she had enjoyed taking care of him, and he was always kind and polite and didn't harass the nurses like some of the older grumps did. She spoke of his prayer life and how he would wheel around in his chair and offer to pray with anyone who wanted a prayer. She even presented my mother with a beautiful plaque that all of her staff had signed, and on the plaque was a folded pair of hands, wrapped with rosary beads. There wasn't a dry eye in the house, except my mother. She said, "If anyone expects me to cry, they better put an onion in my handkerchief." The service concluded and we then went to the cemetery, where Norman was buried next to his parents. He was buried with military honors. I was glad and thankful to God, I had shared the Gospel with Norman.

In two thousand and thirteen, we were at a Regan family gathering and I was sitting at the table with my father. He got a little teary-eyed and out of the blue said to me, "The worst mistake I ever made in my life, was the day I left your mother." You could have blown me over with one short breath. I never knew! He continued, "I left because I was ashamed of what I had done to your mother and I was sorry for ever meeting up with Ida. After I was thrown out of Autumn Avenue, I went to my car and screamed for nearly an hour. I had made a huge mistake, but didn't know how to fix it. I talked with Father Bill, but he told me not to worry so much about Harriet, because my marriage wasn't recognized by the Catholic Church, so that helped me walk away." He walked away from Harriet, Emmajoy, Arty and Autumn Ave. He walked away from, and drastically changed our futures. By now we were both too weepy to talk. I had a huge lump in my throat and I felt shaky and sick to my stomach. But he took out a picture from his wallet and showed it to me. "This is a picture of your mother at Paddy and May's wedding. Isn't she beautiful? She was beautiful. I couldn't speak. He said, "Your beautiful smile reminds me so much of your mother. I loved her from the first time he ever saw her."

"Emmajoy, please forgive me for not being a good father to you and Arty. I know I was never there for you two. In my lifetime I could not make up to you, for all the pain I caused. He then asked me, "How is your mother?" and in a soft whisper I said, "She died last winter." All of us, at the table silently wept for several minutes. "I wish I could have been there," he said. I think Harriet wished the same thing. I wept for my mother on that day, more than the day she died.

My Dad became critically ill a couple of years ago and was failing quickly. I knew as a Christian, I had to tell him about Jesus, so I did. I called him on the phone and he was thrilled to hear from me. We were not estranged, but as he aged, we grew closer and closer. In our conversation that evening, he said to me, "I'm very proud of you Emmajoy. You made a wonderful life for you and your family." I told him it would have not been possible without the Lord. He quietly listened as I told him about Jesus. I then asked him if he wanted to accept Jesus, as his own personal Savior as He is the only way to heaven. He said "Yes," and I then prayed with him. Yahoo!! What Redemption! What a gift I should be given here on earth! Me, bringing my father to Christ, knowing he is going to have everlasting life. I told him when he got to heaven, he was going to see my mother. "Yes I am, yes I am," he replied.

A short time after that conversation, he was admitted to the, ICU in his local hospital. I was able to be there to hold his hand while he passed from this earth and went to his final resting place, which is heaven. I put my phone to his ear and played, Patsy Cline singing, "The Tennessee Waltz."

A few days later I had the privilege of officiating at his "Celebration of Life," service in my church building where he was given an, "Irish Firemen's Farewell." I then prayed at his gravesite, knowing he was home at last.

"But as for me, I know that my Redeemer lives." Job 19:25 NLT.

Before Mom died, her body was nearly totally destroyed. In the last year of her life, she could not walk, she barely ate or drank, and she developed a huge bed sore on her coccyx from sitting. When my sister got married, my son had to carry her from the truck to the front row. This was caused by her lifetime of two packs a day. I once tried to calculate how much money she had spent on cigarettes in her lifetime, but I got mad and stopped.

She had been in the hospital for a couple of weeks before she died, mostly for comfort measures as we did not want her to suffer. She made herself a full DNR (do not resuscitate), as she wanted nothing done to prevent her death. In the first week she was at the hospital, she ate barely a teaspoon of food a day and drank about the same. We did have intravenous fluids going, as we wanted her to be as comfortable as possible. She was also wearing a bi-pap mask at all times. It seemed she was more comfortable at the hospital than at home.

I went to visit her one afternoon and I knew she knew about Jesus, because after all she is the one who taught me to pray. I told her it was okay to go to heaven and see Jesus if he was calling her home. She answered me with one of her vulgar remarks. I thought, okay, then she's not ready.

She had many visitors, as she had retired from the same hospital she was now dying in. She had retired a few years prior from the Linen Department. Working for the hospital was the only job she ever had and she had worked there for about fifteen years.

One of her nurses suggested we might want to "cut down the visitors" to let her rest. Cut down? No, that wasn't going to happen. Who would we "cut down" anyway? She had seven children, all married, and all of them had children. In all we were thirty one people with just the immediate family, which included her grandchildren. The same nurse complained we were taking up all the chairs on her unit. I spoke to the manager on the floor and they were able to move her to a two room private area. We were all very grateful. We would have to ask her visitors not to ask her too many questions, as it was difficult for her to talk. Everyone was very compliant and kind. My church family made sure there was food in my refrigerator when I came home. And the offers to "help in any way I can," were too numerous to count.

A week passed, and the hospital wanted to place Mom in a Hospice facility. We were certainly agreeing. She had been living with my sister, but the care she needed had reached a professional level.

I arrived in her room one evening after work, and she was more awake than she had been in days. I noticed she had been crying. The only other time in my life I saw my mother cry, was at her mother's funeral. "Mom, are you in pain?" She shook her head no. I jokingly said, "Is it something I said?" She smiled and shook her head no. I just let her rest, as I knew how much energy it took for her to speak. I sat there that night and sang her many songs. I sang old church hymns, I sang her songs she liked from the 40's. I sang for nearly two hours. I reminisced out loud and reminded her of the good family times we had. I then kissed her on her forehead and said goodnight.

Mom was not a kisser, hugger or a teller of I love you, until later in life. I do remember her telling me she loved me when I was a small child, but I always had to say it first. Through her whole life she seemed void of emotion, except anger. For Mom anger was exposed loud and often. If you did catch her at a tender moment she would say, "Ah."

Her depression had destroyed her early and midlife years. It ate her up and those years were gone. I only saw Mom come out of her depression later in life when she had her seventh child, her fifth son. After his birth, she stayed up! She washed clothes, made food and cleaned her house. She took taxies to visit her sisters. She truly fell totally in love with her new son. He was a preemie. They named him, Edward Jude Fitzgerald. He was only seven months younger than my daughter, and my son was three years older than him! My Mom and I were pregnant at the same time!

Norman was still drinking his whiskey, when Edward was born, but we were all so much older, his sins didn't have as much effect on us and many of us were out of their house altogether. We were all concerned for Edward, but Mom seemed to "step up" and she protected this tiny tot from his father. If he came home drunk and tried to harass Edward, Mom would tell Norman, to, "Back off," and he did. She was also totally in love with my children and they could do no wrong in her eyes, and eventually as they were all born, none of her grandchildren could do wrong. She had the true Grandmother's love.

It was Friday morning and my sister called me on the phone to tell me to get to the hospital, right away. I stopped what I was doing and rushed to the hospital seven miles away. My sister met me in the hallway and said, "Mom is dying and she needs you to help her go to Jesus, because she doesn't know how. She told me to call you right away, so I did." I assured her she had done the right thing. What better gift in life could I receive? I sat at her bedside, and I said to her, "Mom, do you believe in Jesus?" She shook her head yes. "Do you believe He is the Son of God?" She shook her head yes. "Do you believe you are a sinner and He can forgive you?" She shook her head yes. "Do you want Jesus to be your Lord and take you to heaven?" She shook her head yes. I told her, "You now know Jesus!" She let out a complete sigh and she was totally peaceful.

I stayed with her for the rest of the day and she started to moan in pain. I asked her if she was in pain and she shook her head yes and pointed to her abdomen. I asked her if she wanted something for pain and she shook her head yes. We then decided it was time to her give something, but it had to be IV, because at this point she was unable to swallow. An hour after she had the morphine put up, she lifted her face mask off, looked me straight in the eye and whispered, "I'm sorry." It nearly broke my heart. I couldn't hold back the tears, not because she was dying, but because she was, "Sorry." That "sorry" spoke to her failed marriage of Neil, and her abusive marriage to Norman, the abuse of Arty and her other son. It was a sorry for eating the Thanksgiving orange. She was sorry for the neglect of Arty's leg. Her sorry spoke to the countless hours she spent in bed and neglected us. It was a sorry that spoke to her depression and lack of caring. It was a sorry for our hunger. It was a sorry for Arty's urine. It was a sorry that spoke up for missing every school play I ever sang or acted in. It was a sorry for shop-lifting. It was a sorry for diaper rashes. It was a sorry for the life that was taken after Edward was born. It was a sorry that regretted she didn't help me during the times of rats, roaches and roaming hands. It was a sorry that spoke to every swear word that came out of her mouth. It was a sorry that she ever smoked. It was her verbal repentance to God.

At this moment in time, I was closer to her than I had been my whole life. Mom was in a heavenly place, repenting, and the Lord let me in on it! "Call Emmajoy, and tell her to help me go to Jesus." It does not get better than that. I was given a precious gift from God at that time. Mom and I were in His presence. I could tell by the glowing peace on her face. We sat quietly for a while and she fell asleep. She slept for a few hours and when she awoke, she said she saw Aunt Abby, in heaven and she told her she was going to heaven soon. She said Abby was young and pretty, not old and sick. Aunt Abby was Mom's youngest sister, but Aunt Abby was more of a close friend than an aunt. I loved her dearly and I was glad the Lord let me know she was in heaven, because I also shared the Gospel with her before she died, but she always had a deep faith in God.

I could see Mom's body was fading by the hour. I told her, "It's okay to go to go to heaven and leave us, because we will all be okay and Arty will be here in a few hours to see you." She then fell into a coma, and we never heard her speak again. Arty made it to Avon, a few hours later and all seven of us and a few of the adult grandchildren were at her bedside. We sang songs to her as she loved music. We told jokes to her and told her she needed to eat a hot fudge sundae because she was getting too thin. I sang Amazing Grace and my sister collapsed along the wall, my brothers had to pick her up, but I didn't stop singing, but Mom's heart did. She went to heaven. She weighed eighty-eight pounds at the time of her death. She was seventy-three years old.

We notified all the rest of the family, and they came to the hospital one last time. We then called the funeral home to have them take her away. A couple of days later we had a viewing in the funeral home for a few hours and there were literally hundreds of people that came to her wake. I kept looking at the door thinking my father would show up, "any minute now," but he didn't.

The day after the wake, we had a "Celebration of Life" service, but I felt I couldn't officiate at Moms funeral, so my Pastor, led the service for us and at the same time, Mom was being cremated. He did a wonderful job. We then had a huge meal in the fellowship hall of the church and I brought the baked beans.

Mom's ashes are now scattered in small urns, and the family members who wanted them have them. My youngest granddaughter has a tiny amount in a necklace, which she often wears.

All three of my parents are in heaven, not because of me, as I was only a tool. They are there because of the Work on the Cross of Jesus, the Crucifixion and Resurrection and because of The

Blood of The Lamb. Norman is buried in his family plot, in a local Catholic cemetery. Neil is buried in his wife's family plot, in a city several hundred miles from his hometown, and Harriet's ashes are with her children. What a prodigious effect they all had on the lives of the twelve children they gave life to.

"Some however, did receive Him and believe in Him; so He gave them the right to become God's children." John 1:12, GNB.

At the age of seven I knelt at an altar in The Salvation Army Chapel and gave my life to Christ. Even at that young age, I knew I had a need for God. I thank God, the Holy Spirit doesn't discriminate against age.

I was a very unhappy child, and I hated the way I lived. When I was three years old my father gave me a doll that could be dressed in rags, or in a ballroom dress with beautiful blue sparkling shoes. After I opened that Christmas present, I threw it on one of the dressers, in the hallway on Autumn Ave. I didn't need a doll. I needed a coat and dresses and leggings. It was then that I made an inner vow to myself, that I would not grow up and live poorly. I would have food. I would be warm and I would buy boots and gloves. It was there, "Envy" was birthed in my soul. Was my soul wounded in the womb, was it from the abandonment from my father? Was it from the lack of love and affection? Was it from jealousy of other intact families? As my childhood years passed in my life, my soul melted from pain. My self-worth was nonexistent and I thought I was dreadfully ugly. I thought this, because this was how I felt. I felt dirty and dumb. At the age of twelve I was full of anger, envy and shame, and I carried the burden of caring for my siblings. My "Anger" said, don't worry, just protect yourself at all costs. "Shame," told me everything that happened to my family was my fault and "Burden," told me if I didn't take care of things, I wasn't doing my job. "Envy" made me full of bitterness, hostility and hate. I never would want to be that child again.

At the age of twenty-two, I again said the sinner's prayer and asked The Lord back into my life. By this time, I was full of rage and unforgiveness. I don't know how my husband put up with me. The abuse I suffered as a child affected every area of my life. I had trouble giving and receiving love. I didn't trust anyone and I was judgmental and bossy. I once tried to tell a clergy member about some of the abuses I had as a child, and he told me it was okay if I had experienced pleasure from the roaming hands! Really, Really, I was SEVEN years old. He then went on to tell me the more you stir about your childhood, the more it's going to surface dirt to the top of the pot. Another clergy shared with his group of leaders what I had told him in confidence about my abuse. I felt totally betrayed by them. I was looking for help. I wanted to be free from the nightmares, and thoughts that visited my mind on a daily basis. But, unfortunately they were incapable of knowing how my soul was aching. From that point on I never spoke to anyone about my abuse again. I only cried out to God! He listened.

I started to study the Bible and listen to every sermon I could, especially the sermons on forgiveness. The plan of the Devil is to involve you in someone else's sin, and destroy both of you in the process, and it was working. The original sin of another's abuse was not my sin, but the path of destruction it led me down, totally belonged to me. Shame, Burden, Anger, Envy, and Fear, were totally mine. If I had sought help from a medical perspective, I would have been in counseling and medicated for years. But I chose not to take that path because I knew there was nothing impossible with God. I read God's word, I knew it. I believed it and I wanted to live in freedom with God. I was a willing soldier, but I was so, so wounded.

So I stared a life of Worship and Praise. I started a prayer life. I started to join in Godly circles with other Christian sisters. I attended a local church and became an active member. I could see and feel God's hand and love turn my own thoughts and heart around. I saw Him bring order and life, where there had been chaos and death.

For those of us who know God, we supernaturally understand and know how He works. For those who don't know God, they will never know or believe any transformation in life. Either way it is okay, because I know who God is. I press on and don't look behind, because God has my life-plan.

God has called me to forgive. Now one could say, are you crazy, perhaps your parents deserve to rot in hell. They are guilty of abuse, neglect, abandonment, hatred, drunkenness, and on and on. I once thought the same thing. But now I live by a different standard and am responsible to walk like Christ walked. That is, in love. So if I walk in love I forgive. My parent's sins were between them and God. My job is to be obedient to the Word of God. I stopped asking the, "Why Me" question.

I have learned forgiveness is not a feeling, it is an act in faith that says, I no longer hold you responsible for_____ (fill in the blank). It is an act that I had to repeat for years, before I knew of its full impact. Forgiveness is what Jesus gave me, far be it from me, to not extend it to another. Forgiveness changed me, and in a small way changed the world. I enjoy freedom. I enjoy helping others. I especially love leading others to Christ. I love being an influence. I love influencing the outcome! Besides forgiveness helps the wicked memories fade away. Forgiveness can restore dignity, peace and honor.

Don't wait for forgiveness to drop into your lap, because I don't think that's going to happen. But instead, surrender to God what is God's, which is sin. After all, He is the one who sent His son to the Cross for it. Walking from victim to victory is often a painful process, but the joy that comes at the end is immeasurable. Forgiveness is one of the greatest gifts we can give and receive for ourselves. Forgiveness even sets you free to forgive the Clergy. After all they are just men and women. Don't leave the package of forgiveness wrapped up, open it and put it to good use.

Now I cannot go back and change what happened in my childhood and to my flesh, but I have changed my thoughts, my soul and the Lord Himself has renewed my spirit. I once was filled with accelerated hatred which controlled my mind and actions. But according to the Word of God, nothing justifies hatred. Not even child abuse.

In 1979 the house on Autumn Avenue, burned down to the ground, and to this day the lot lies barren. I thank God I never have to see that house again.

I have given to the Lord my Burden, Anger, Sadness and Envy. In turn, He has given me a new BASE. That base is the, "Solid Rock." All other ground is sinking sand. He gave back to me Emmajoy!

Give to the Lord, your so called, "dirty laundry." After all, He created Adam from the dust of the earth, and great crops come from dirt. I know He can make a new life for you. Start your journey anew today. Commit your life to Jesus Christ and forgive. I promise you, you will not be sorry.

> *"I will give you a new heart and put a new spirit in you; I will remove from you your heart of stone and give you a heart of flesh." Ezekiel 36:26 NIV.*

Blessings,
Mary E. Krol, AKA Emmajoy

# About the Author

Mary E. Krol, lives in the beautiful Hudson Valley not far from New York City. She and her husband have a son and a daughter and four grandchildren. She is a born again Christian and is very active in her local church. Mary is also a Registered Nurse.

She is a key note speaker and enjoys helping others grow in Christ. She also moves in the gift of Prophecy.

She can be reached by e-mail at marye.krol@gmail.com

# REFLECTIONS ON THE FOUR R'S OF EMMAJOY

FROM THE FIRST PARAGRAPH I WAS DRAWN INTO Emmajoy's story. It was engaging, fascinating and an enjoyable read. Mary writes with raw honesty and vivid detail, culminating in a whopping ending everyone needs to embrace.

Claire M., Brooklyn NY

The Four R's of Emmajoy is truly a story of redemption. It is a testimony of the resilience of the human spirit, the power of forgiveness and the mercy of God. This book caused me to think about how we tend to judge people without even knowing their story. While many would fold under such abuse, Emmajoy became a strong example of love, forgiveness and stability in chaos. This book will both break your heart and boost your spirit.

Lynda W., Newburgh NY

CPSIA information can be obtained
at www.ICGtesting.com
Printed in the USA
BVHW042129300919
559835BV00008B/73/P